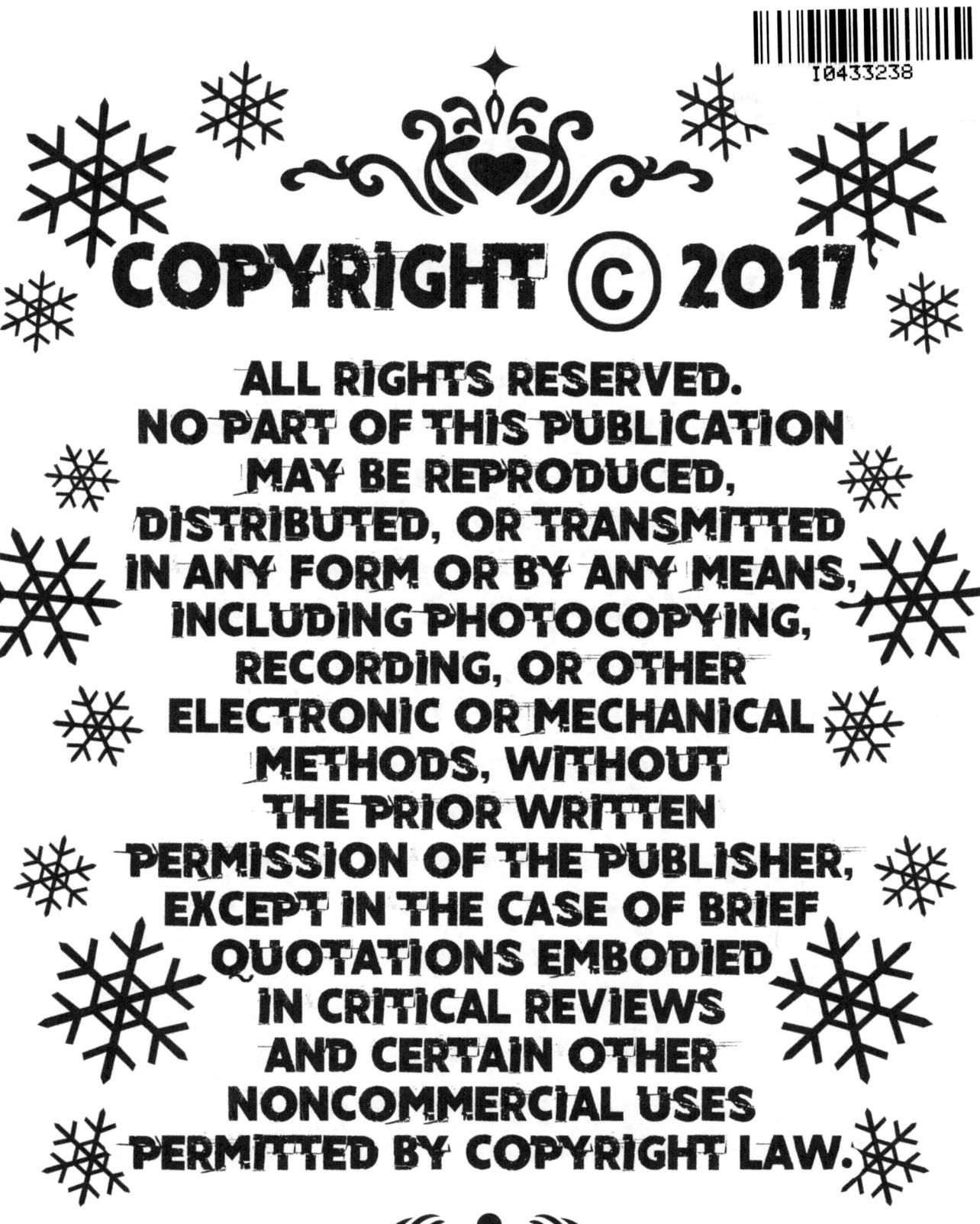

COPYRIGHT © 2017

ALL RIGHTS RESERVED.
NO PART OF THIS PUBLICATION
MAY BE REPRODUCED,
DISTRIBUTED, OR TRANSMITTED
IN ANY FORM OR BY ANY MEANS,
INCLUDING PHOTOCOPYING,
RECORDING, OR OTHER
ELECTRONIC OR MECHANICAL
METHODS, WITHOUT
THE PRIOR WRITTEN
PERMISSION OF THE PUBLISHER,
EXCEPT IN THE CASE OF BRIEF
QUOTATIONS EMBODIED
IN CRITICAL REVIEWS
AND CERTAIN OTHER
NONCOMMERCIAL USES
PERMITTED BY COPYRIGHT LAW.

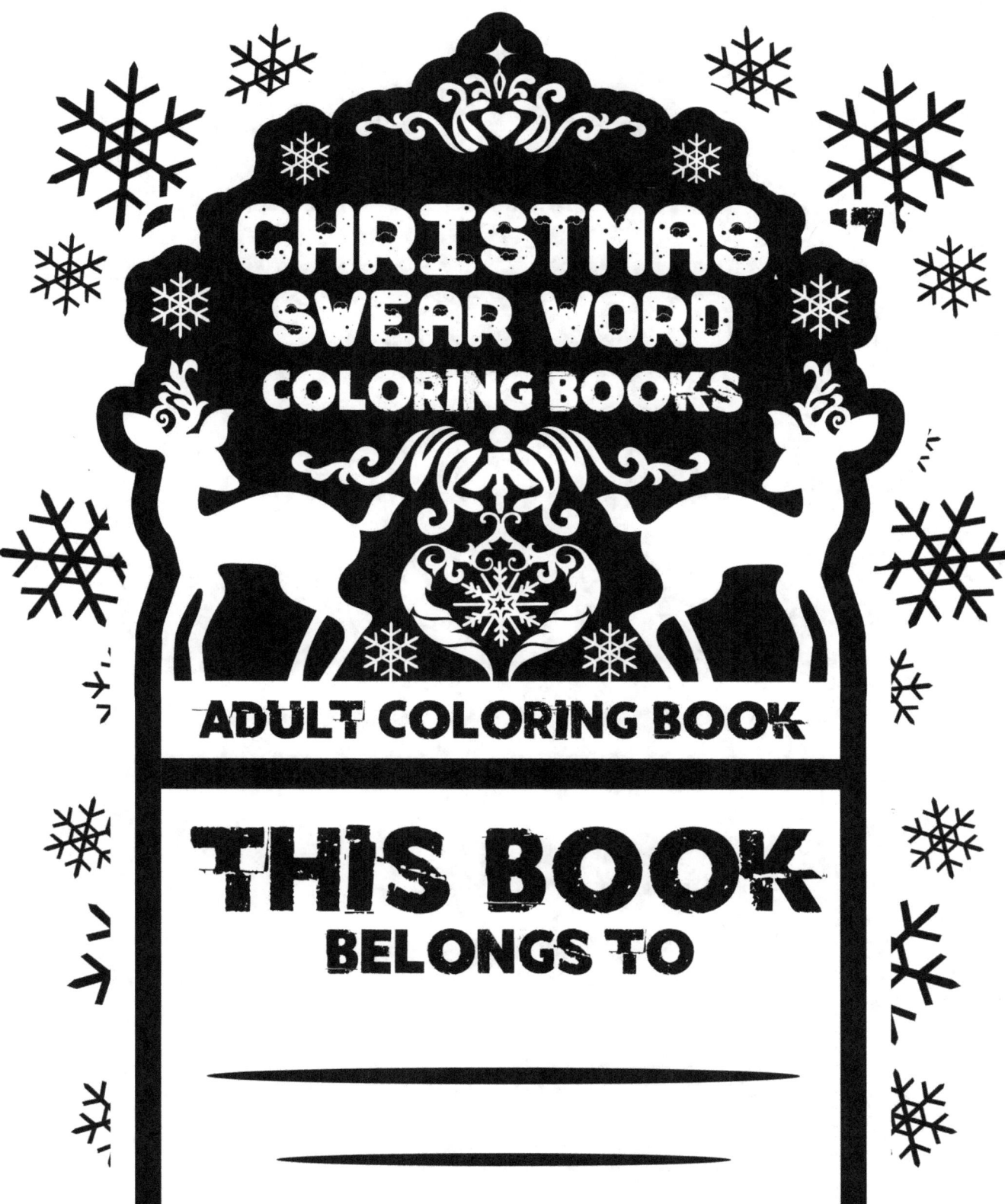

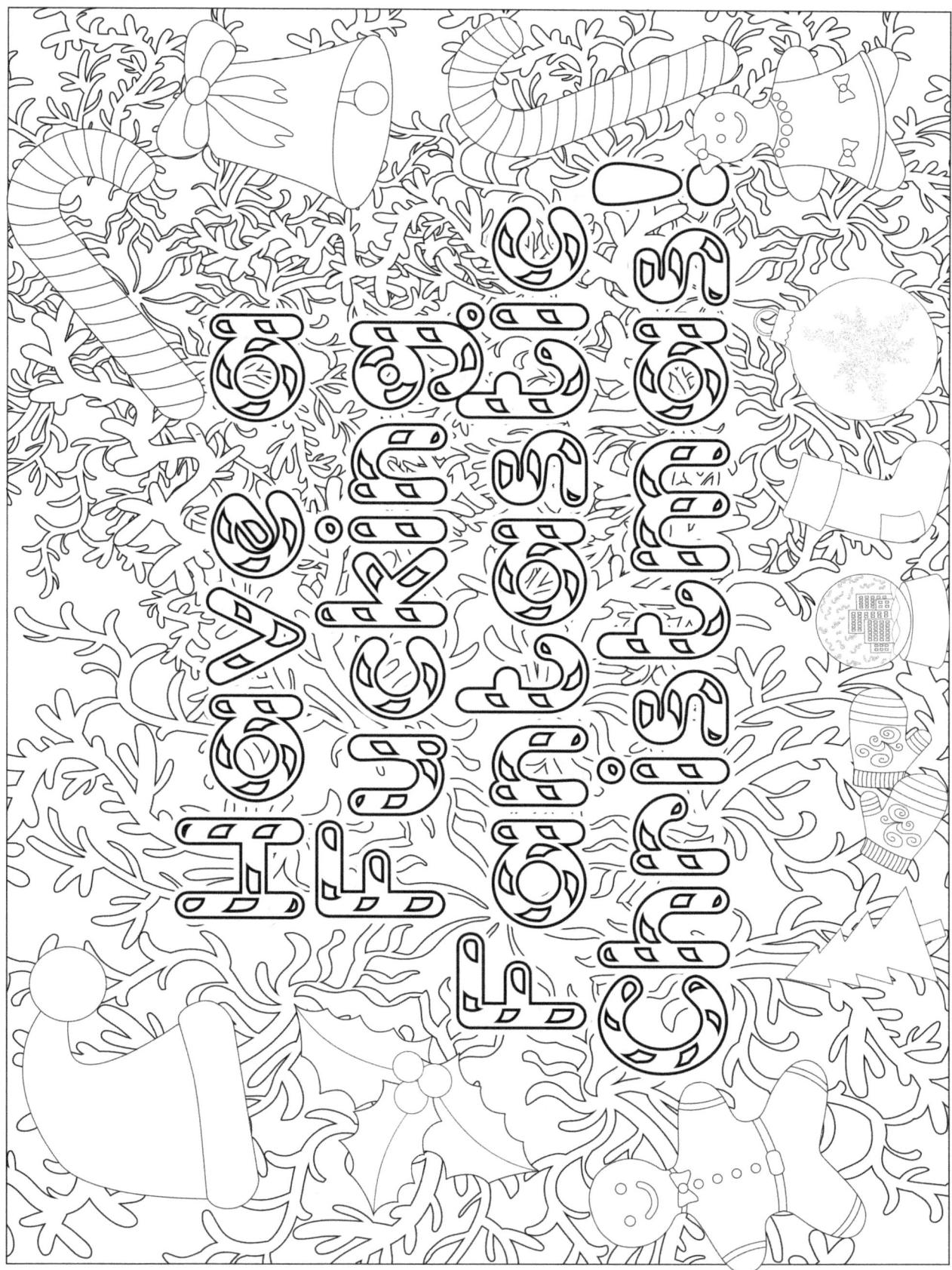

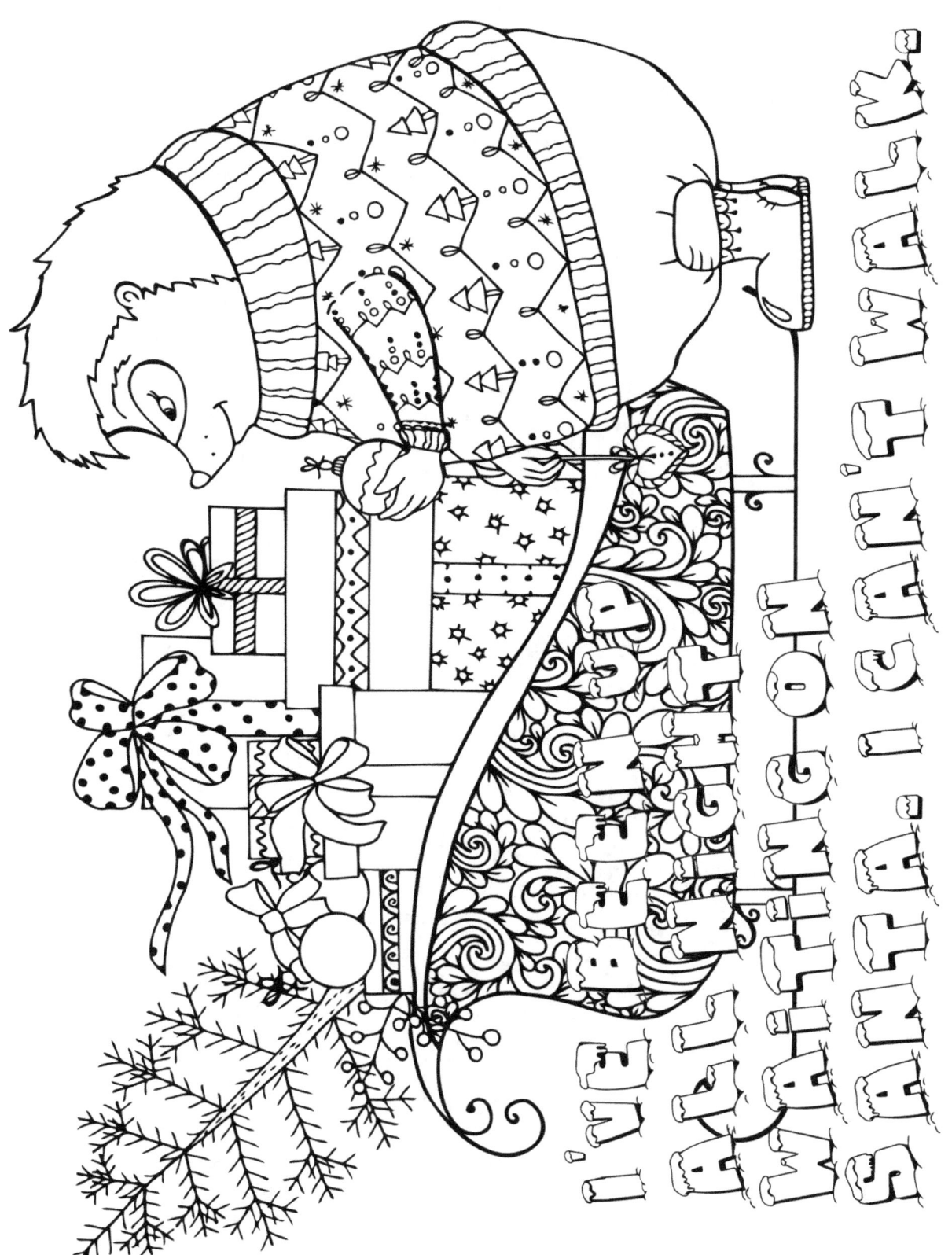

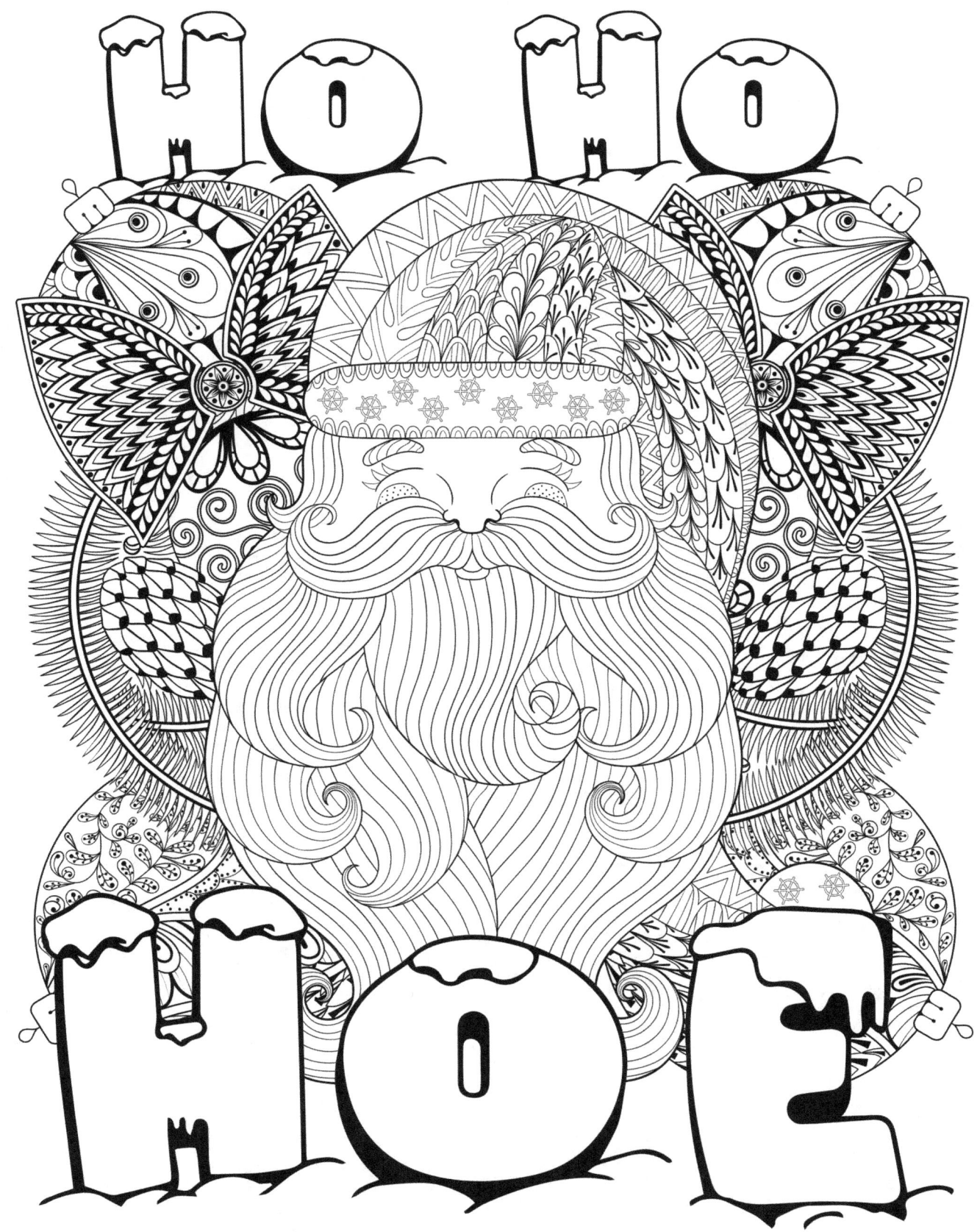

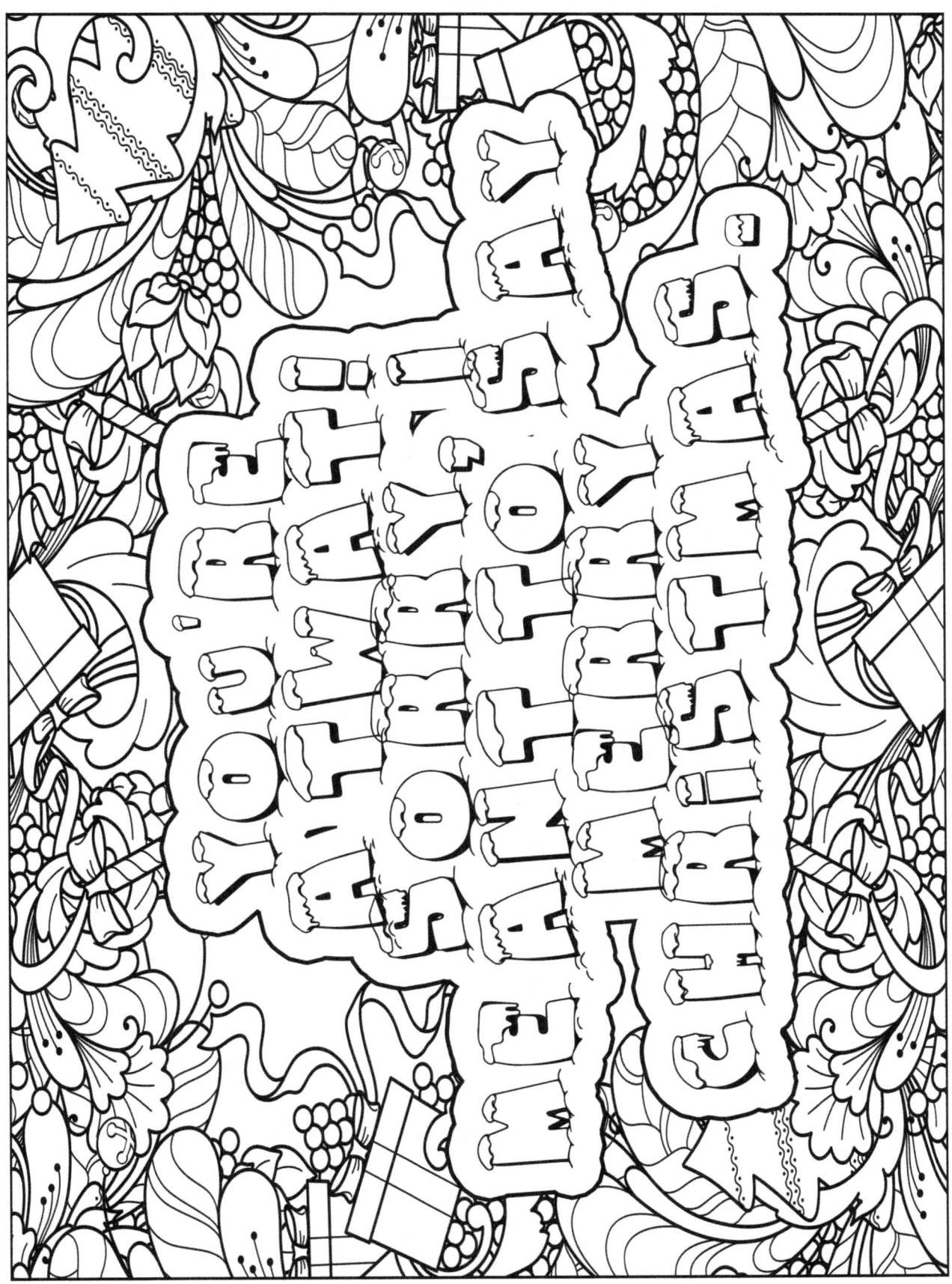

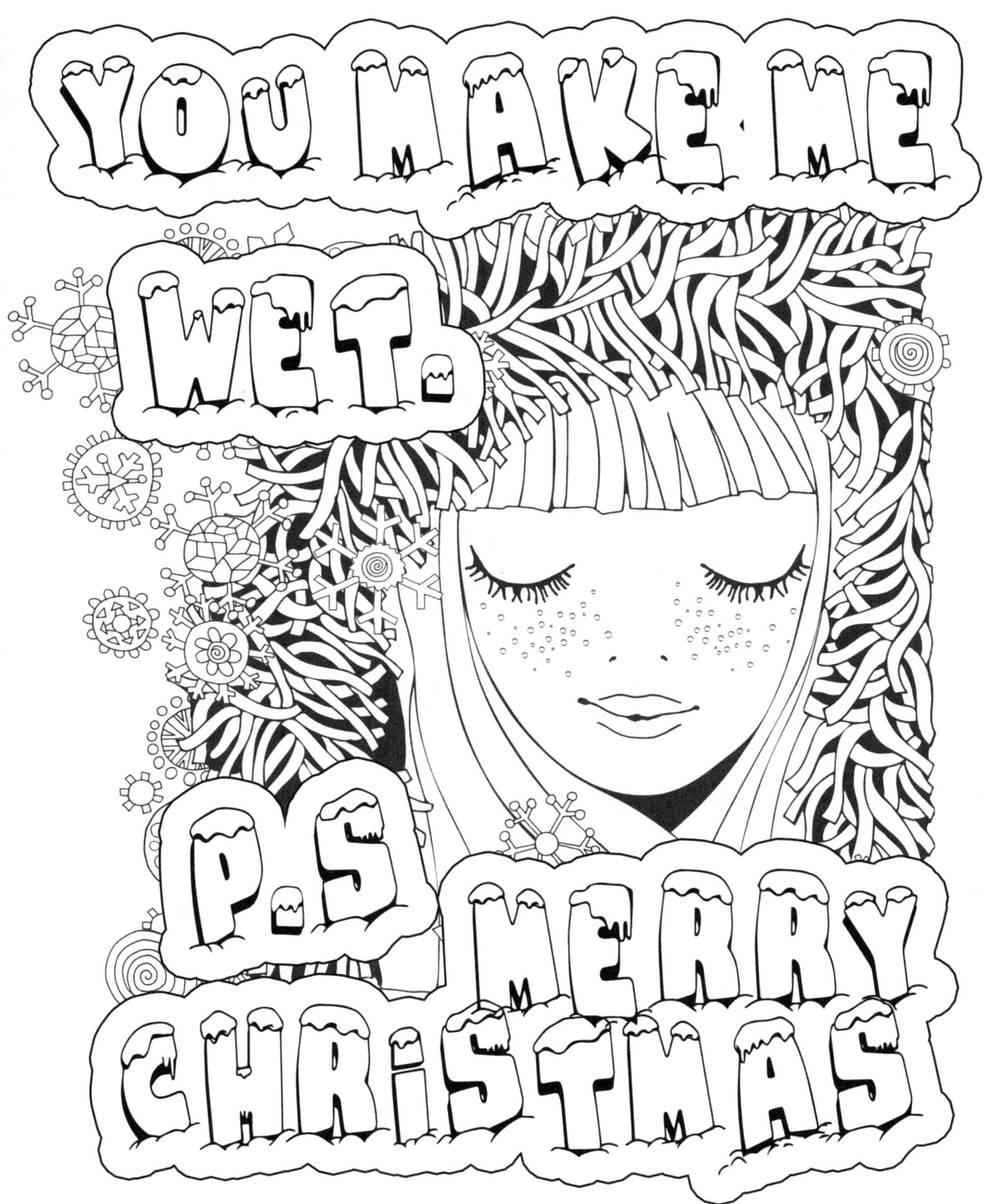

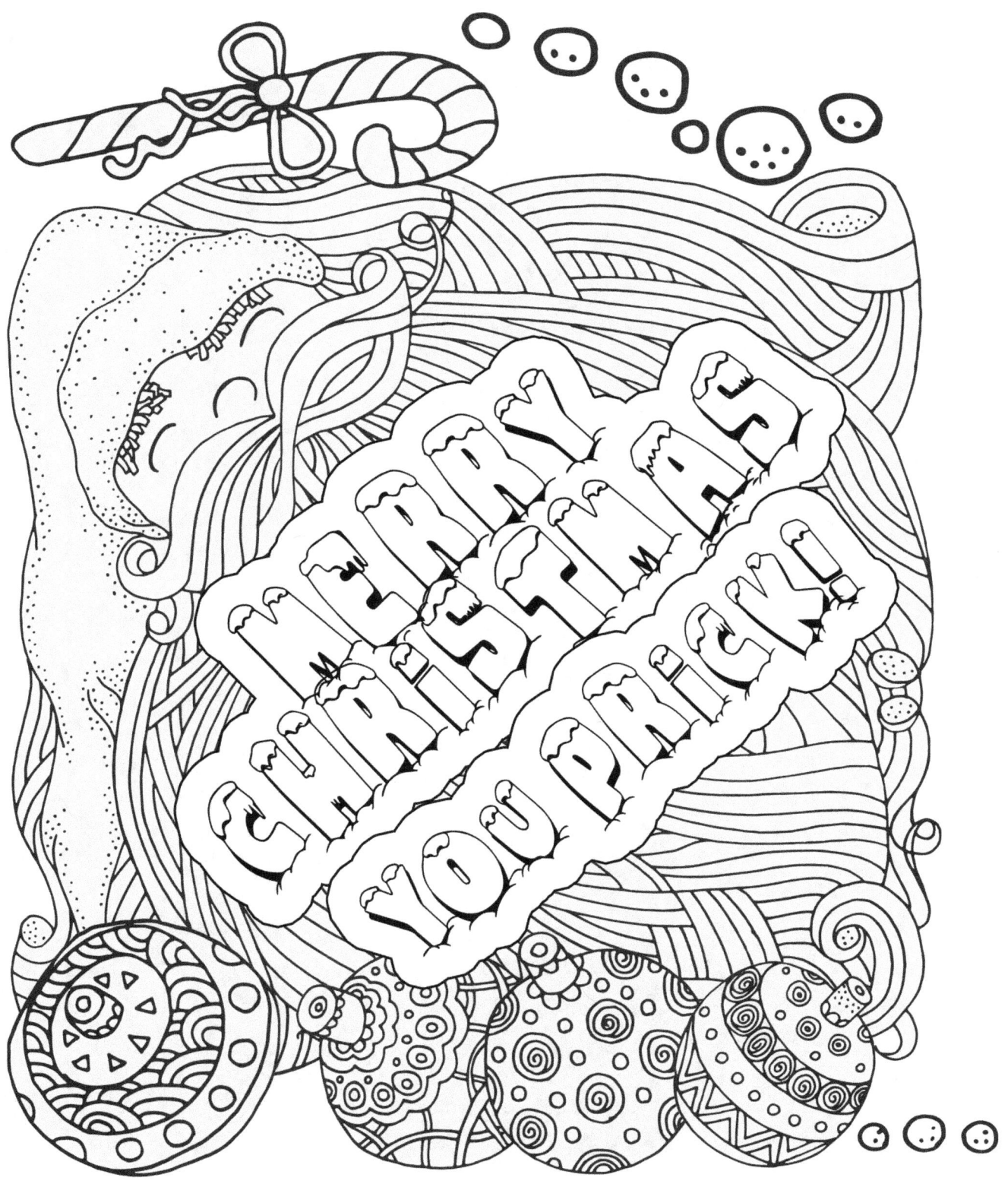

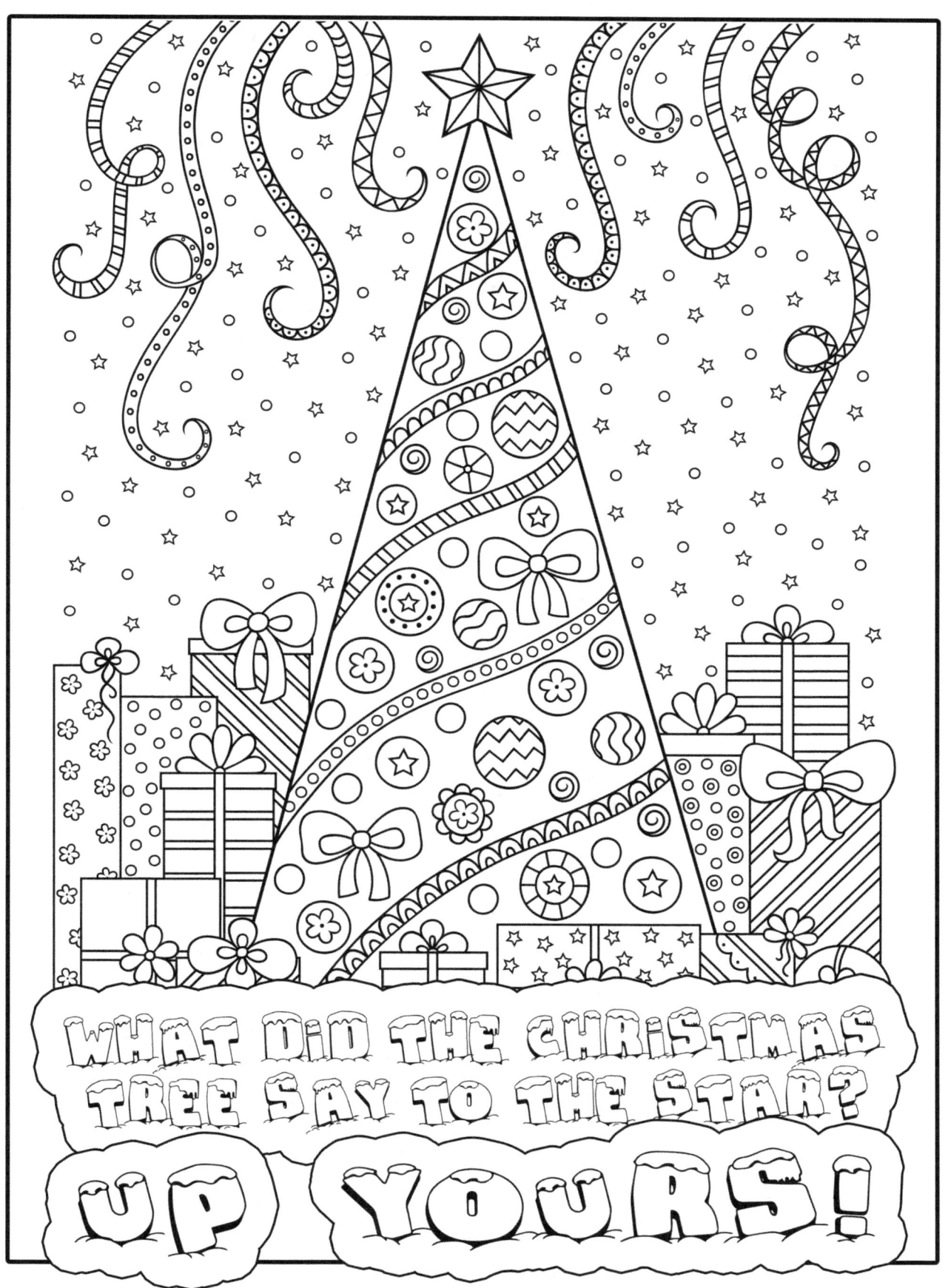

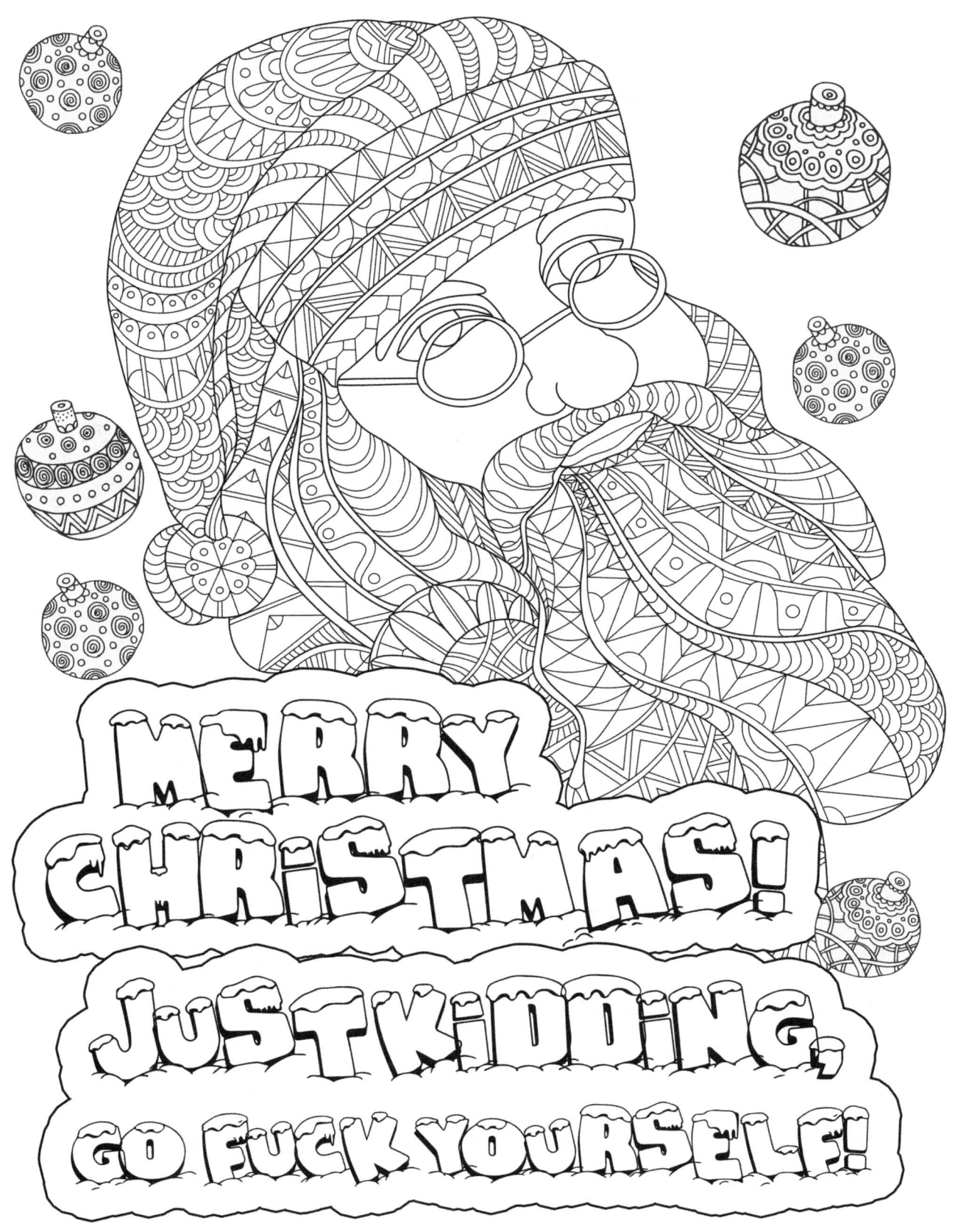

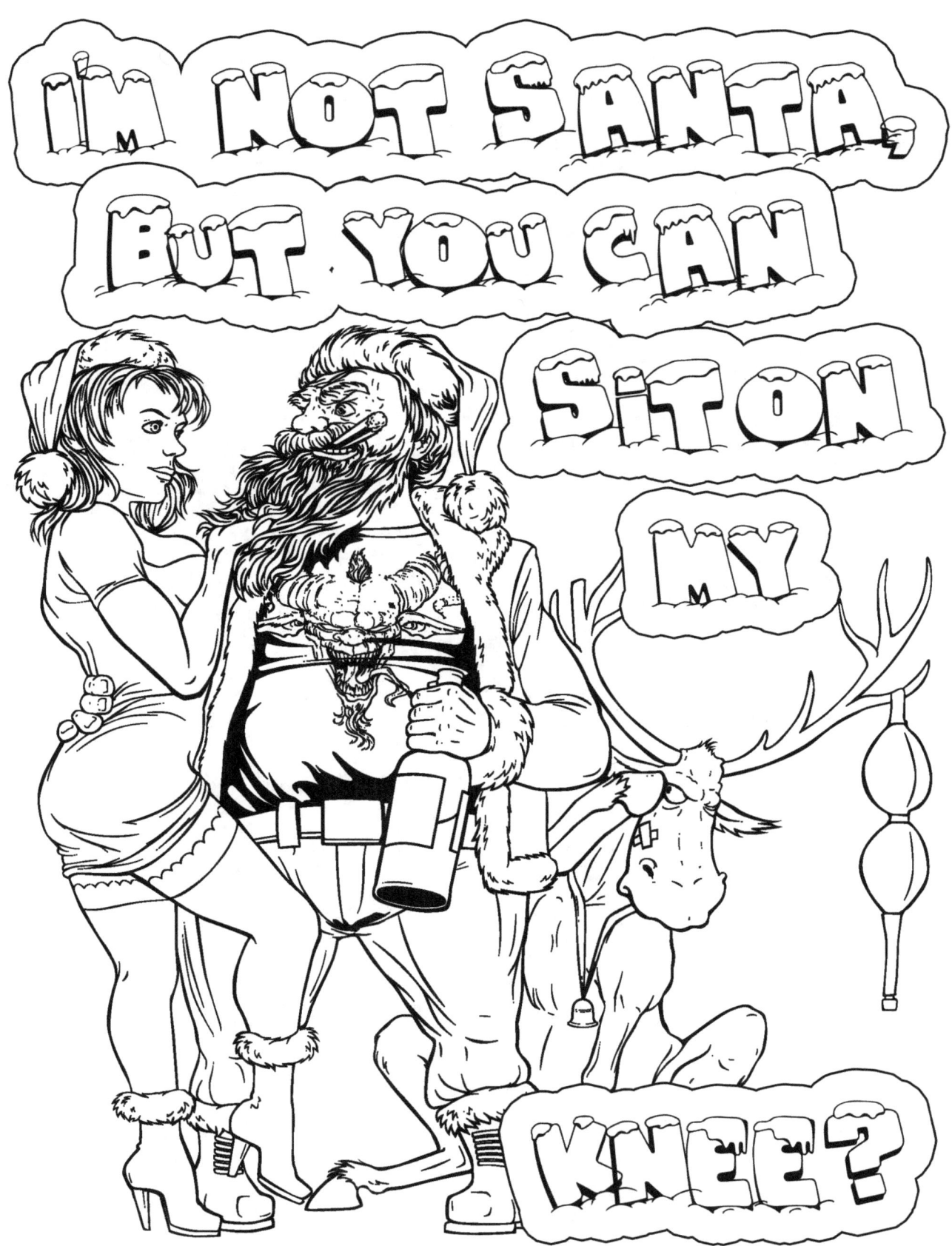

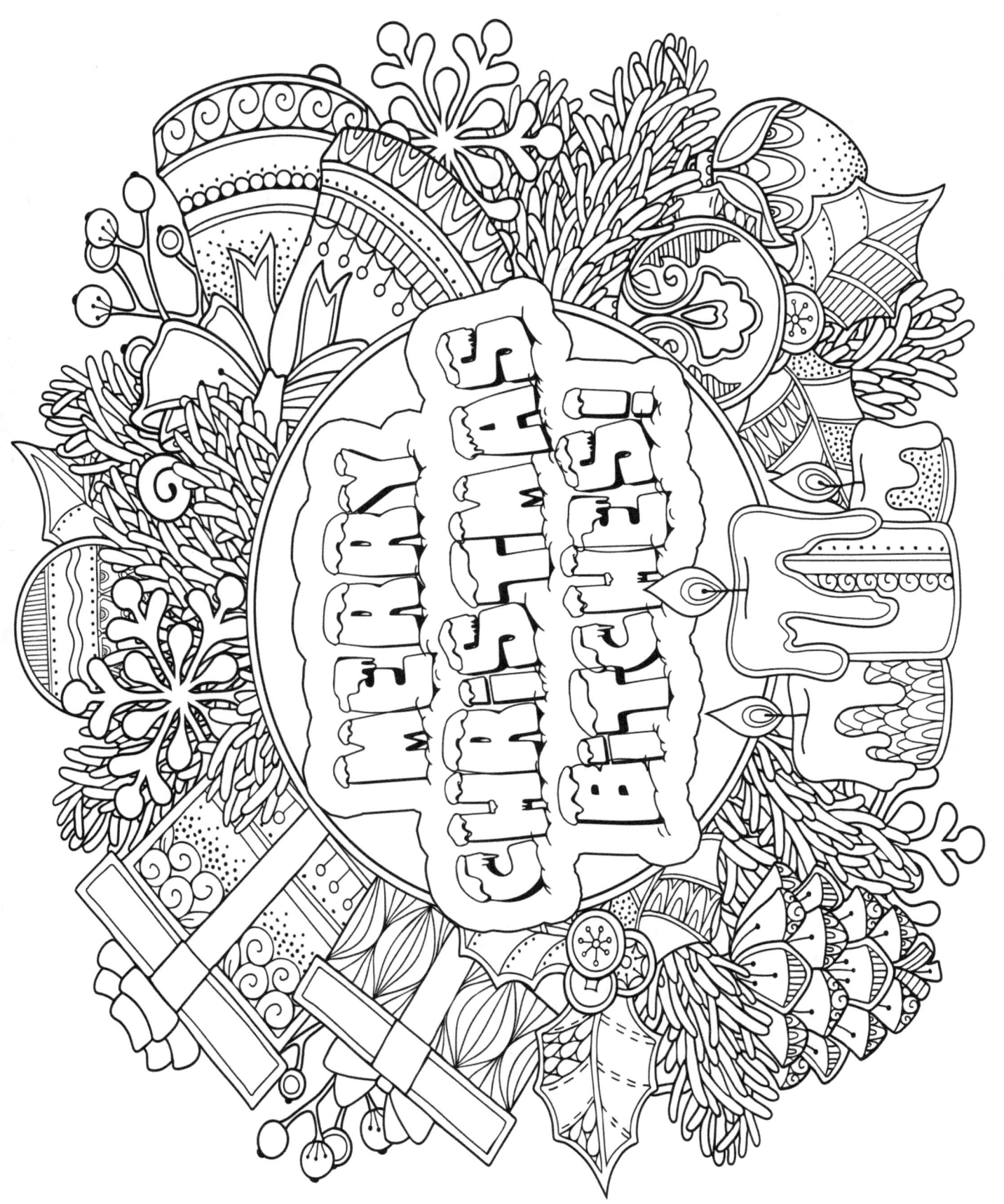

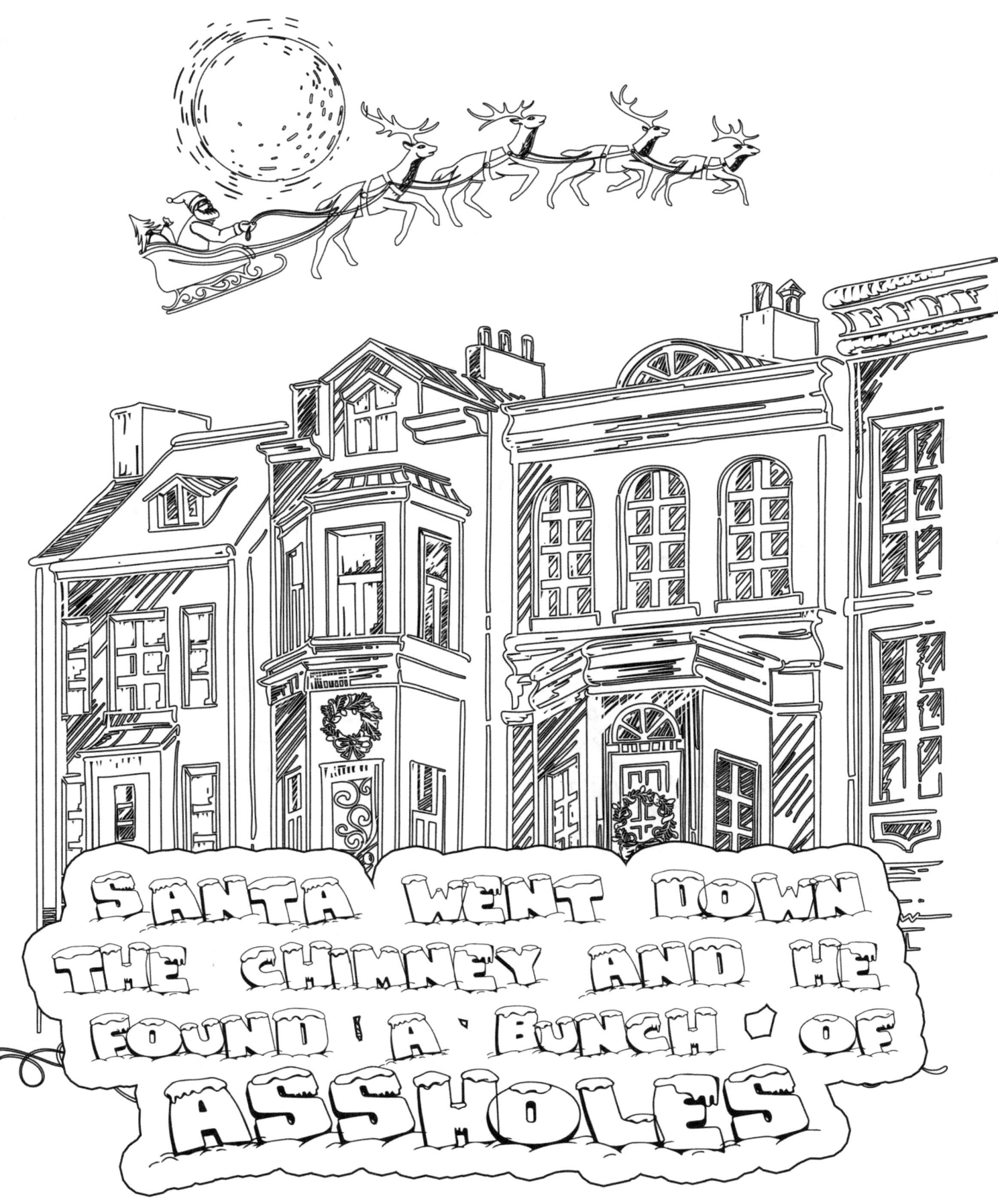

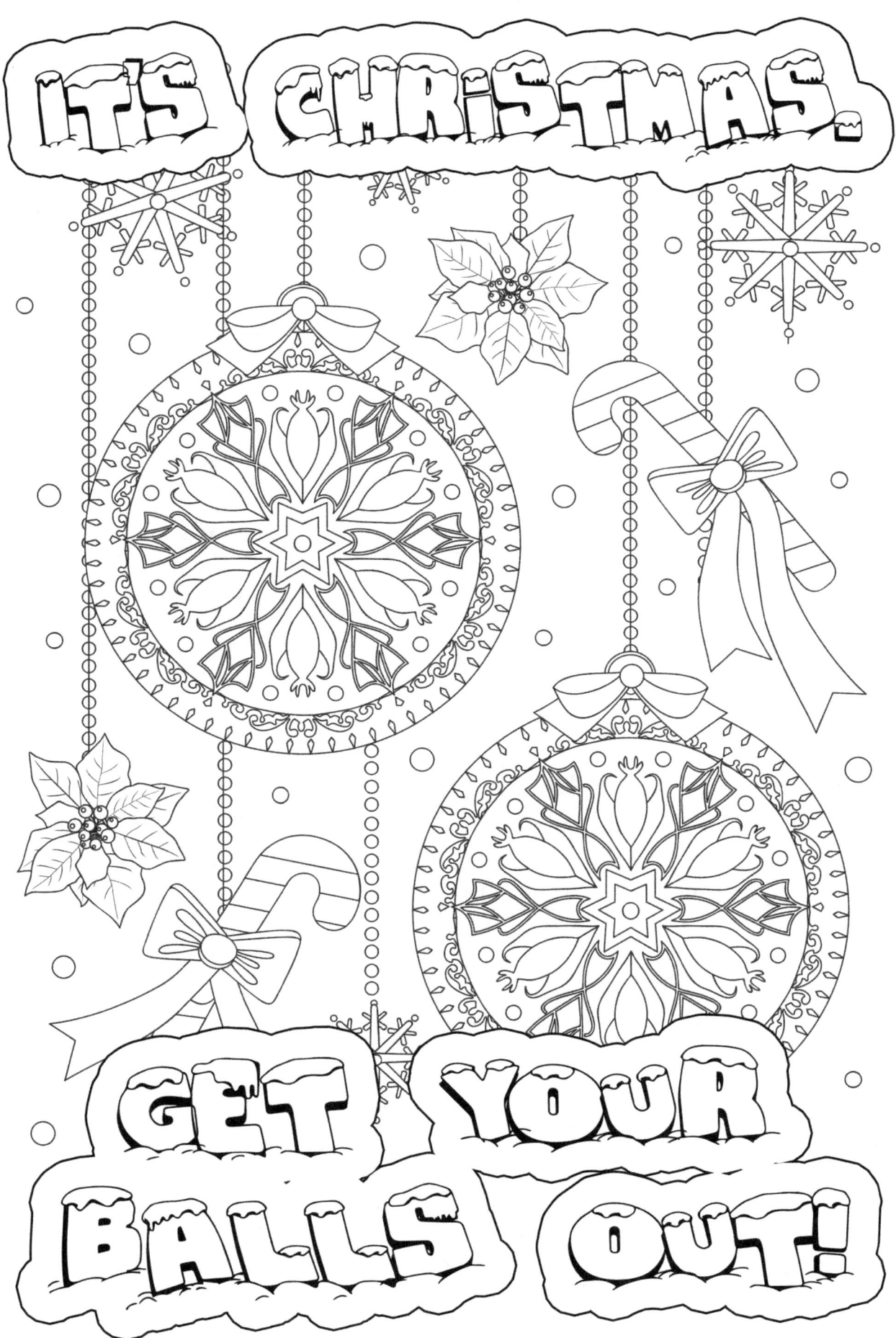

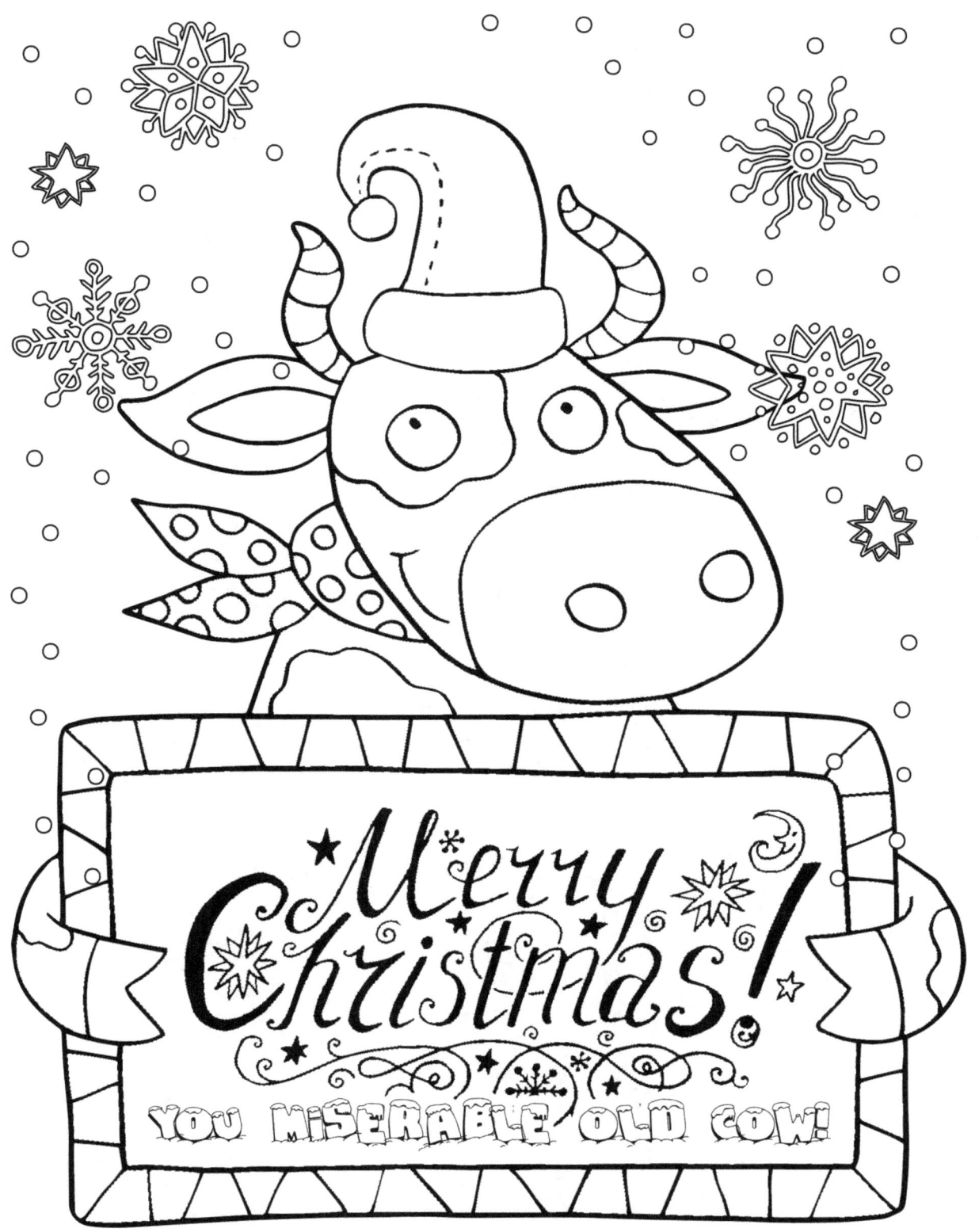

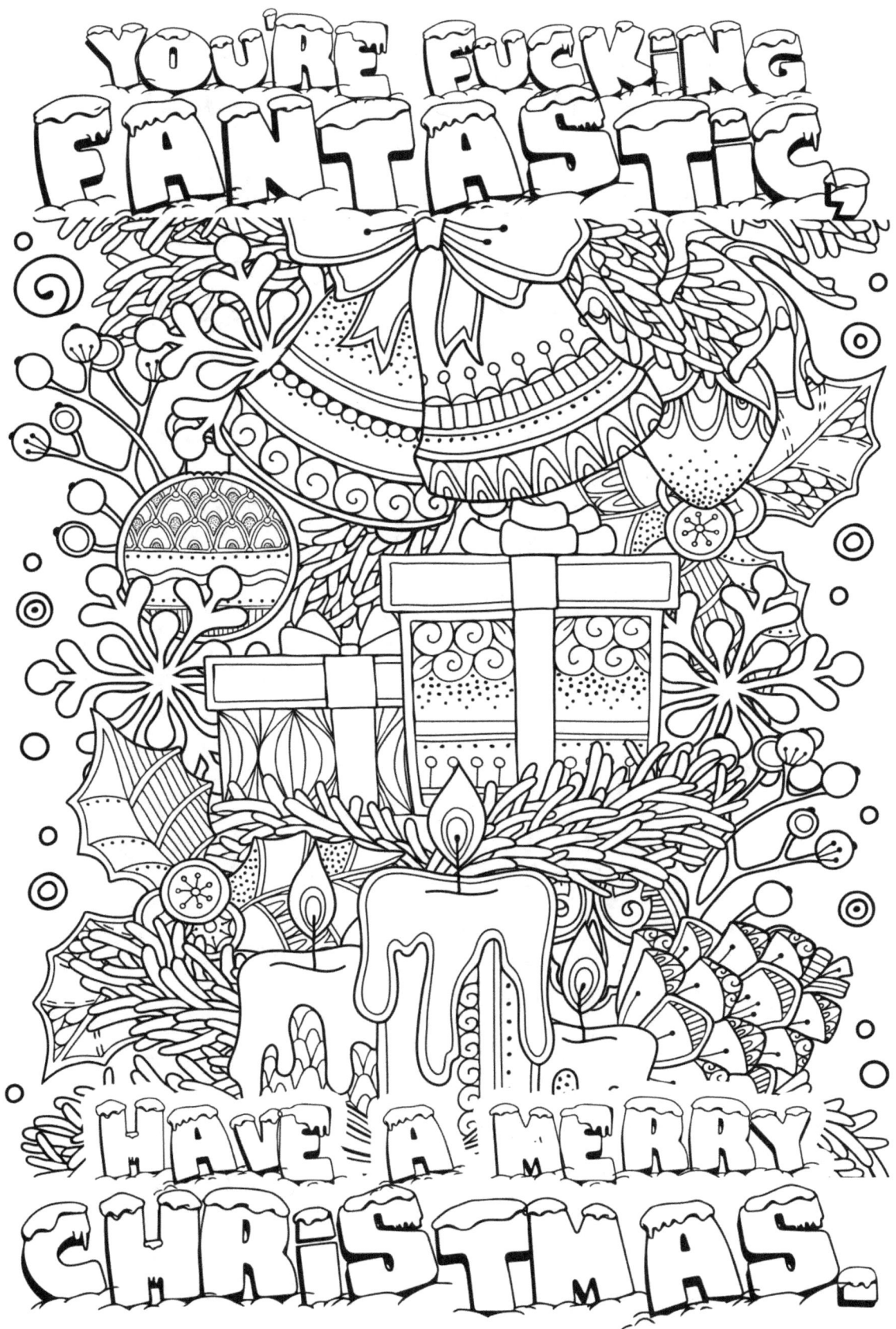

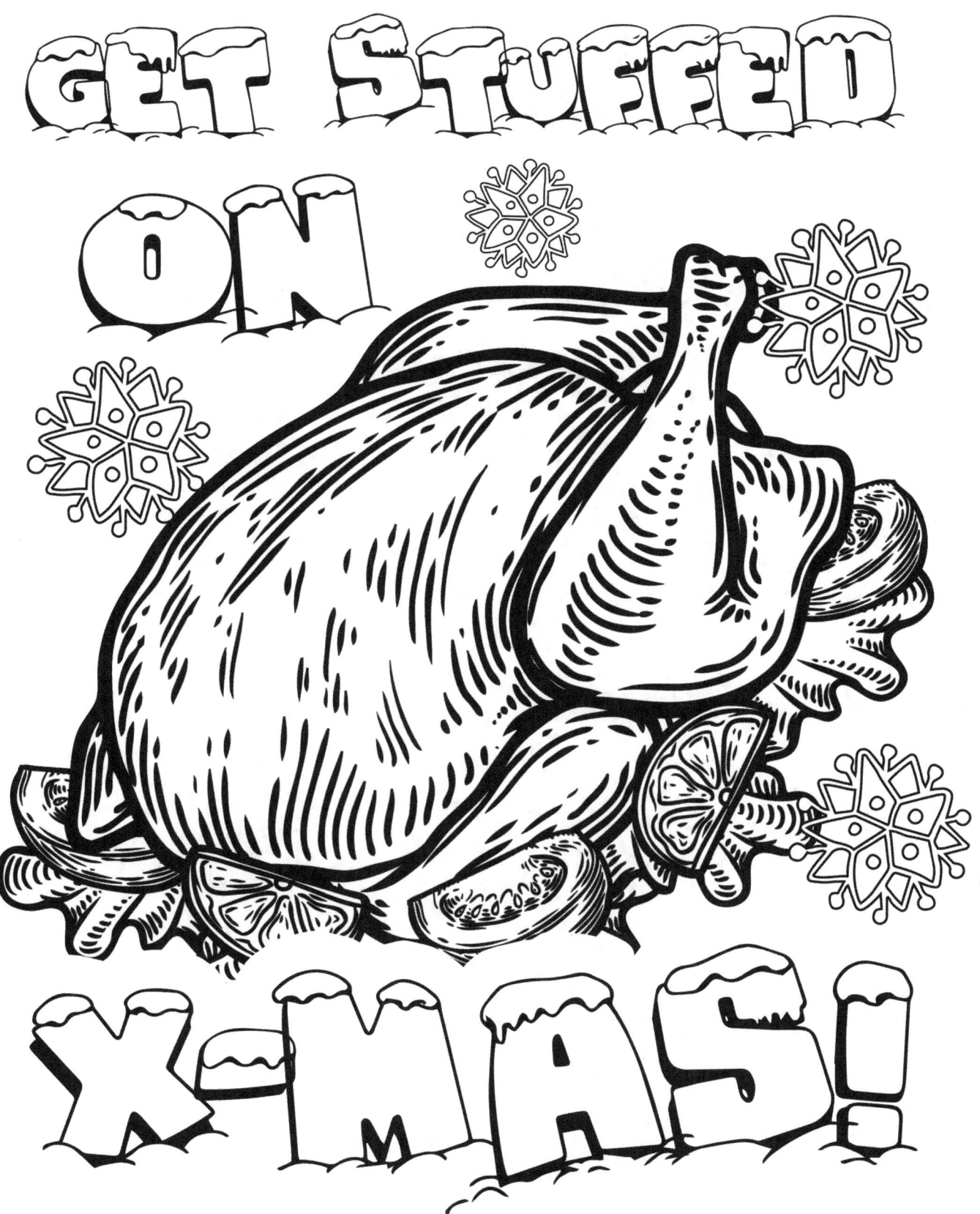

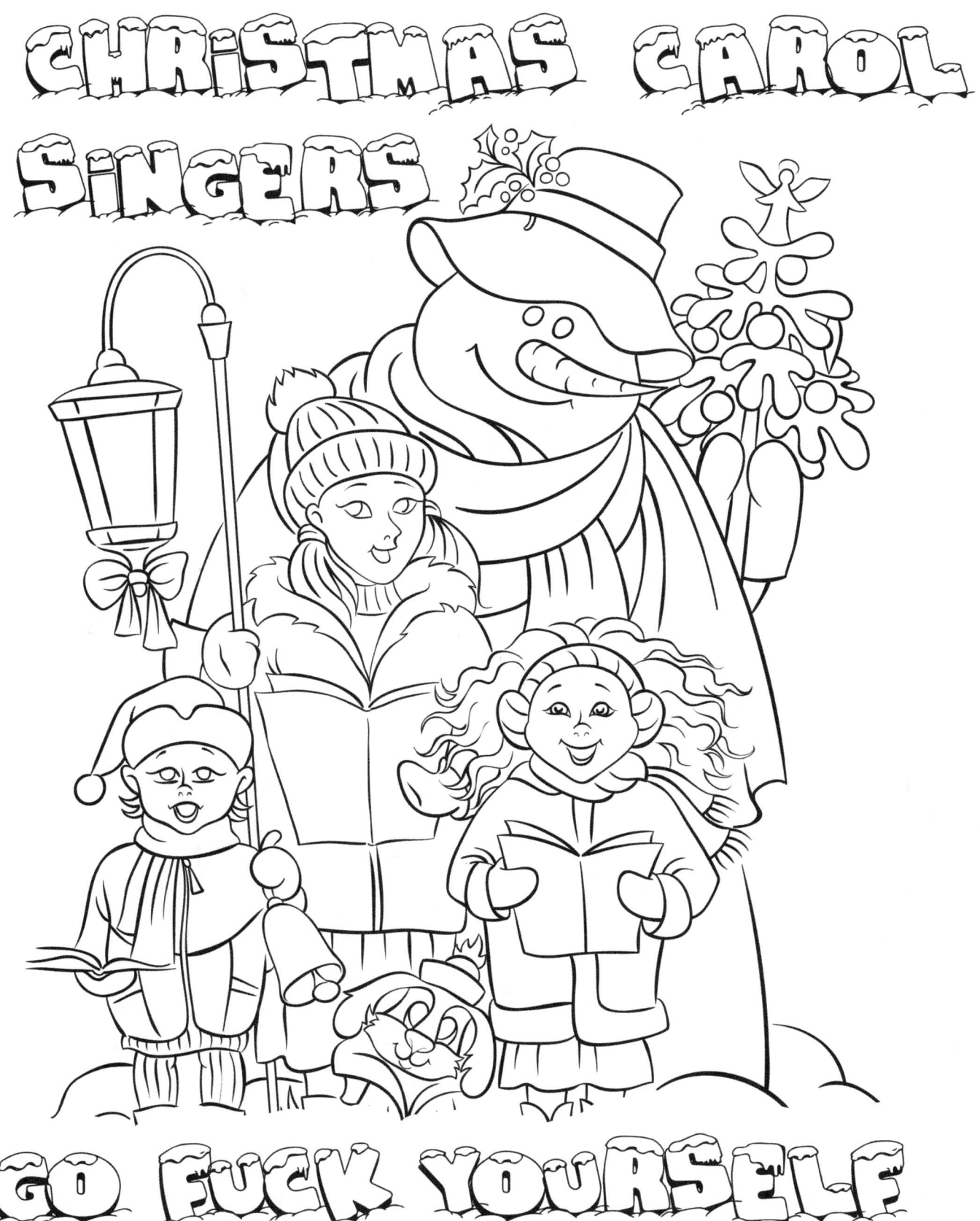

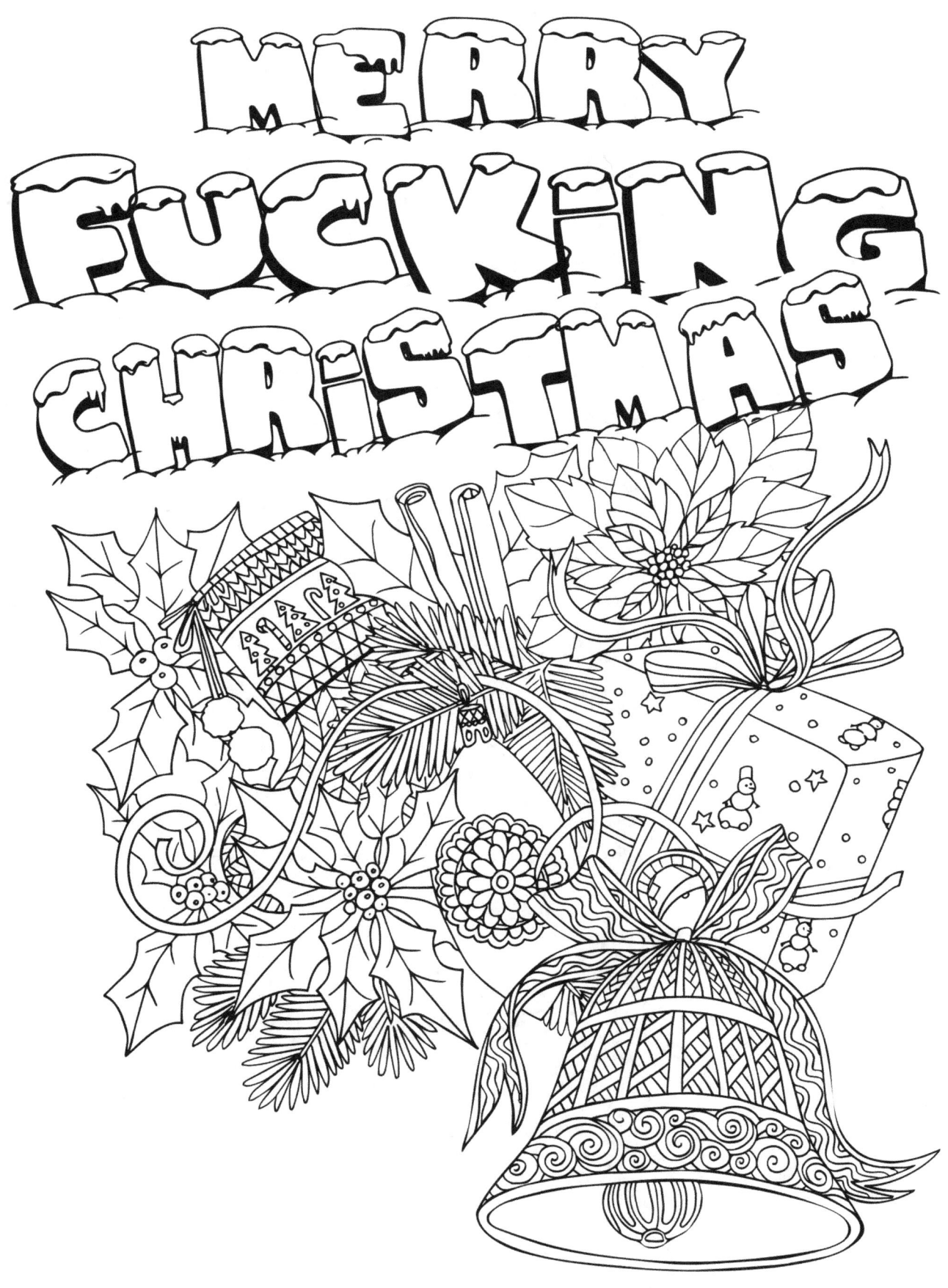

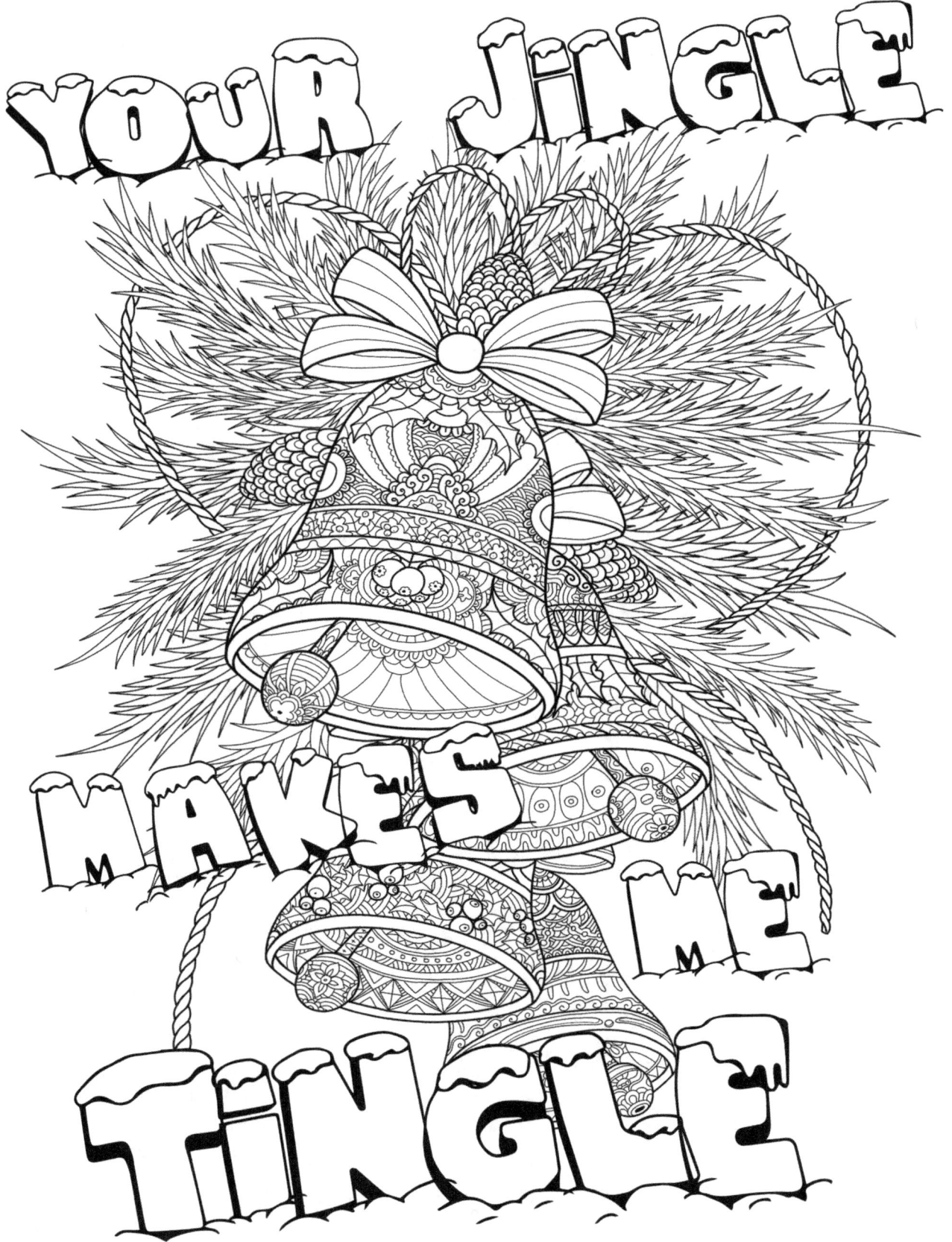

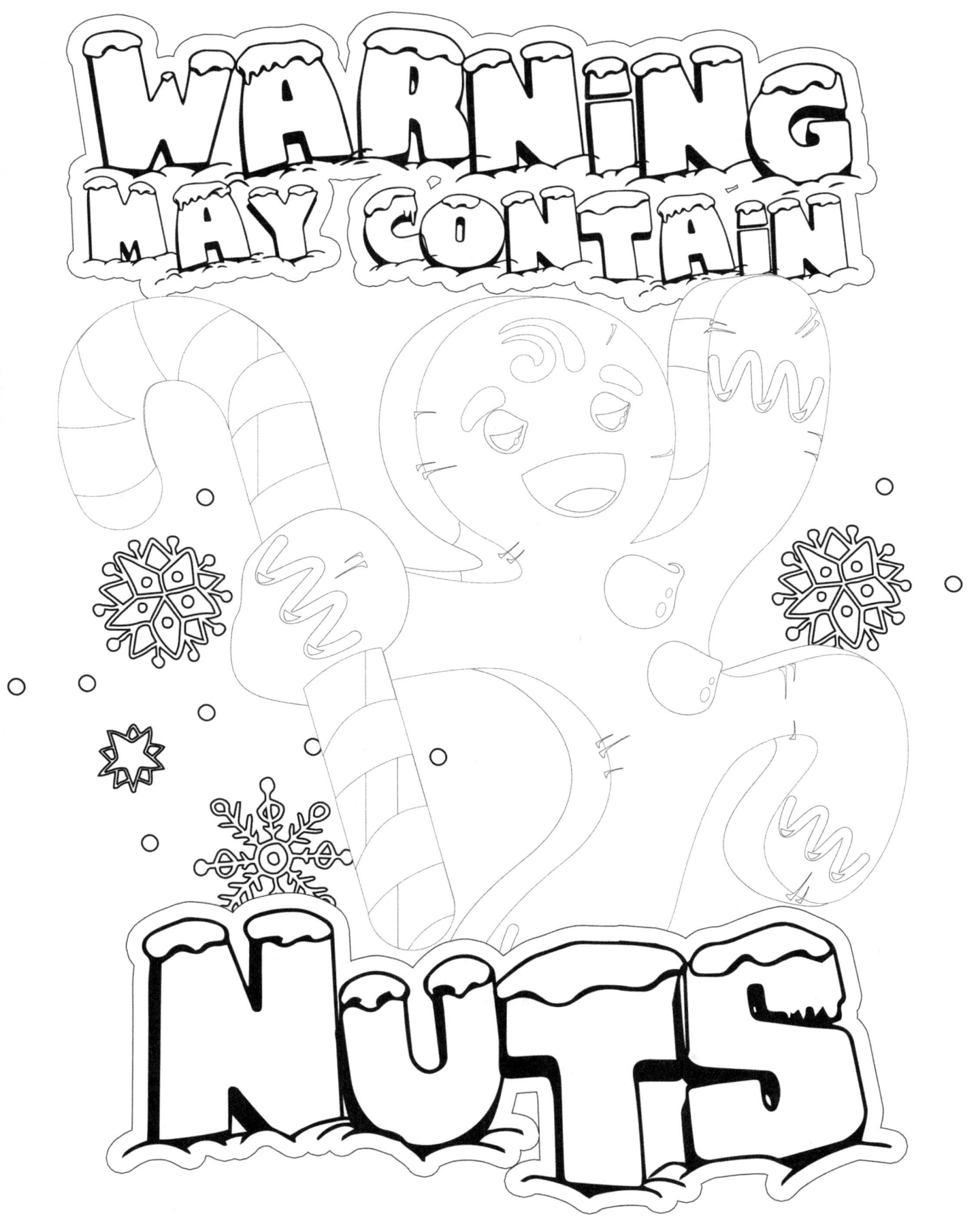

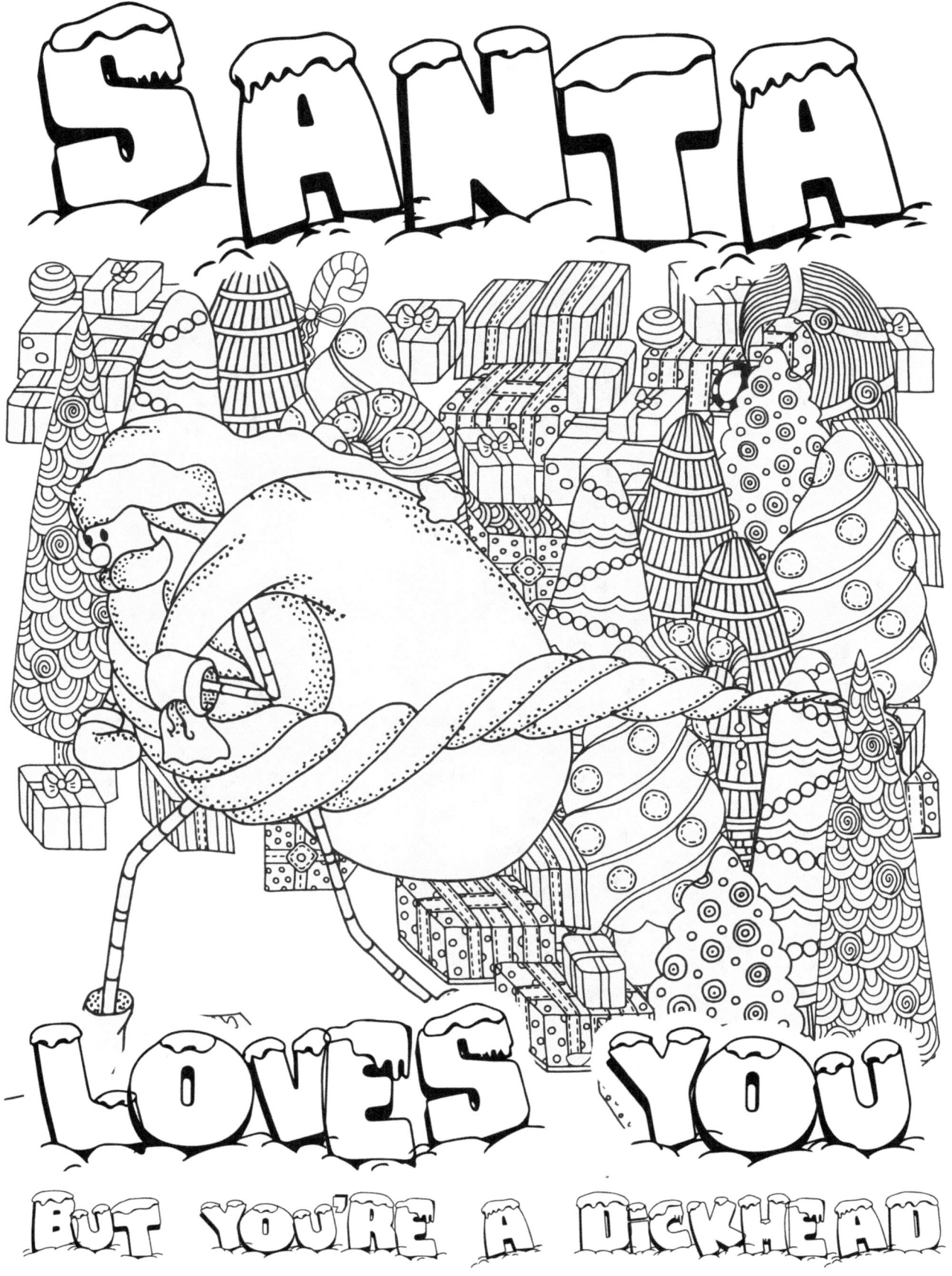

Jingle Bell, Jingle Bell, Jingle Bell... Fuck!

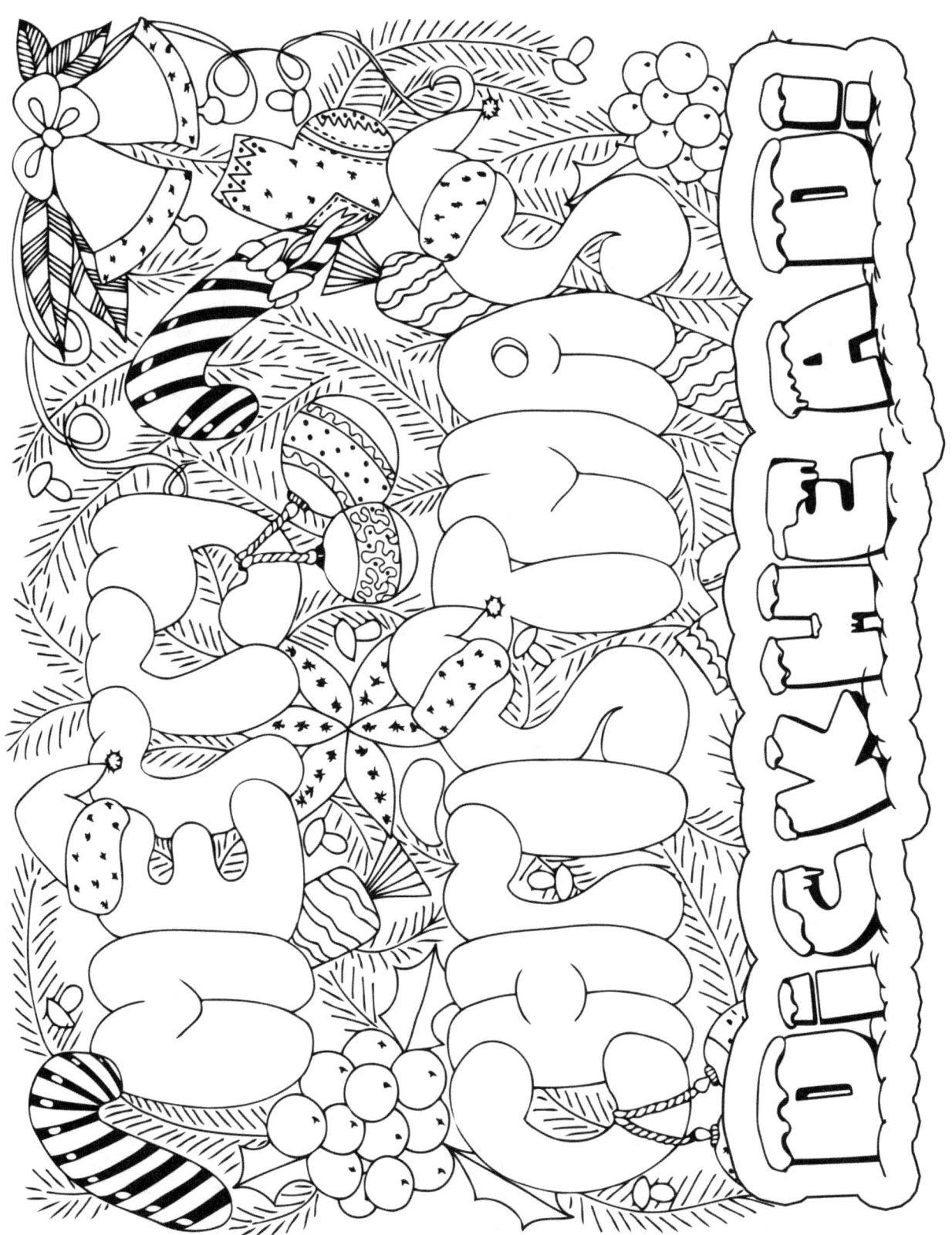

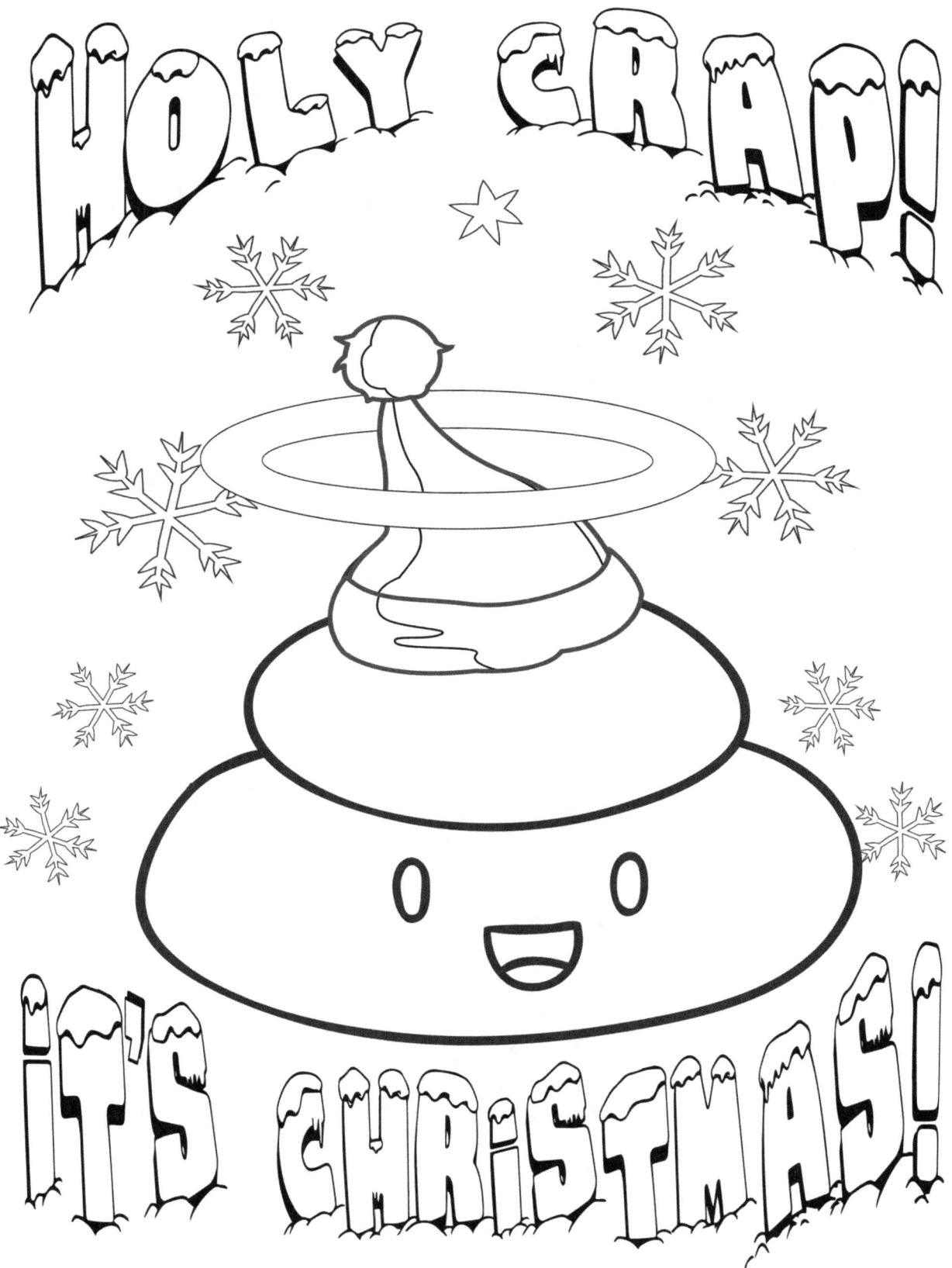

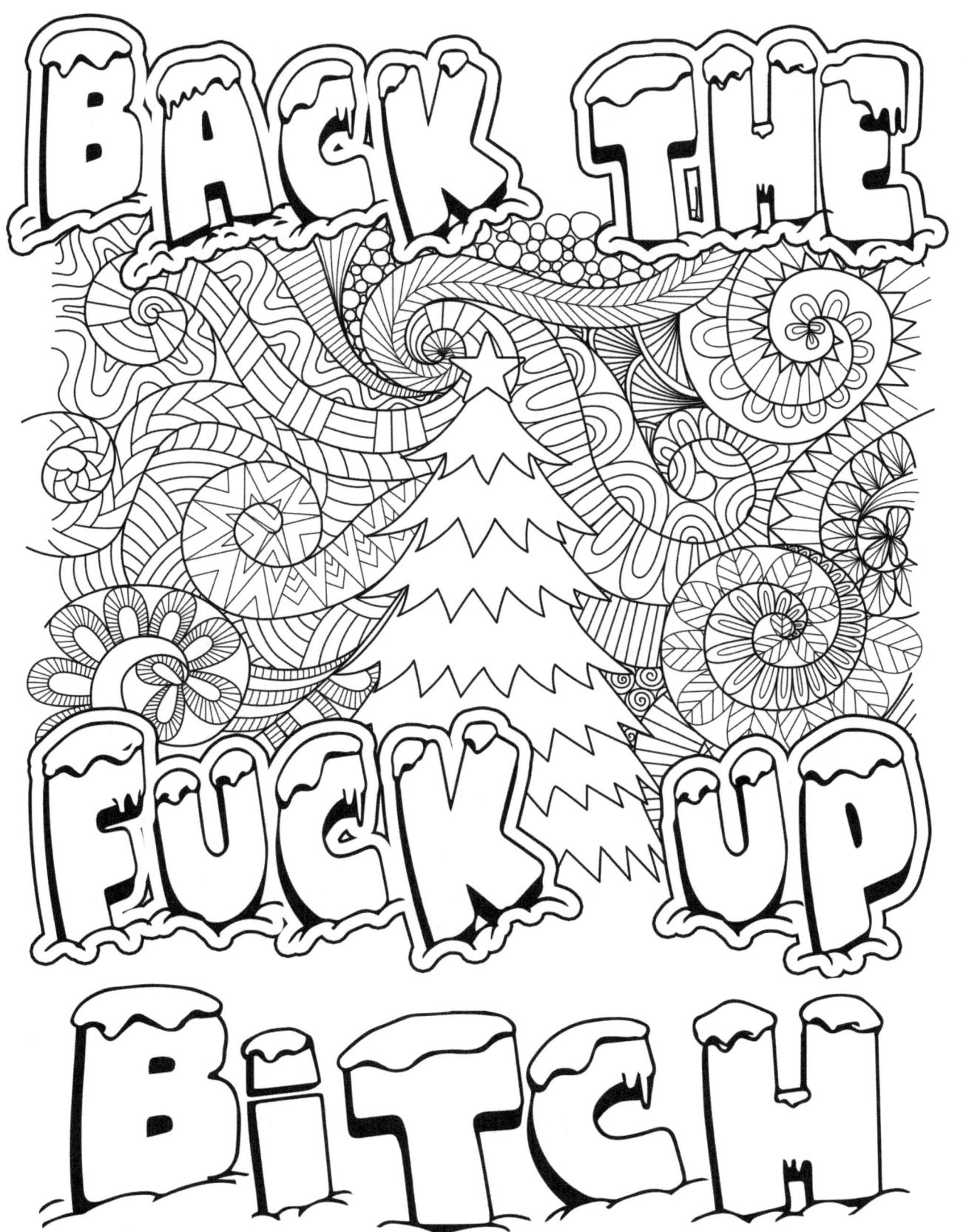

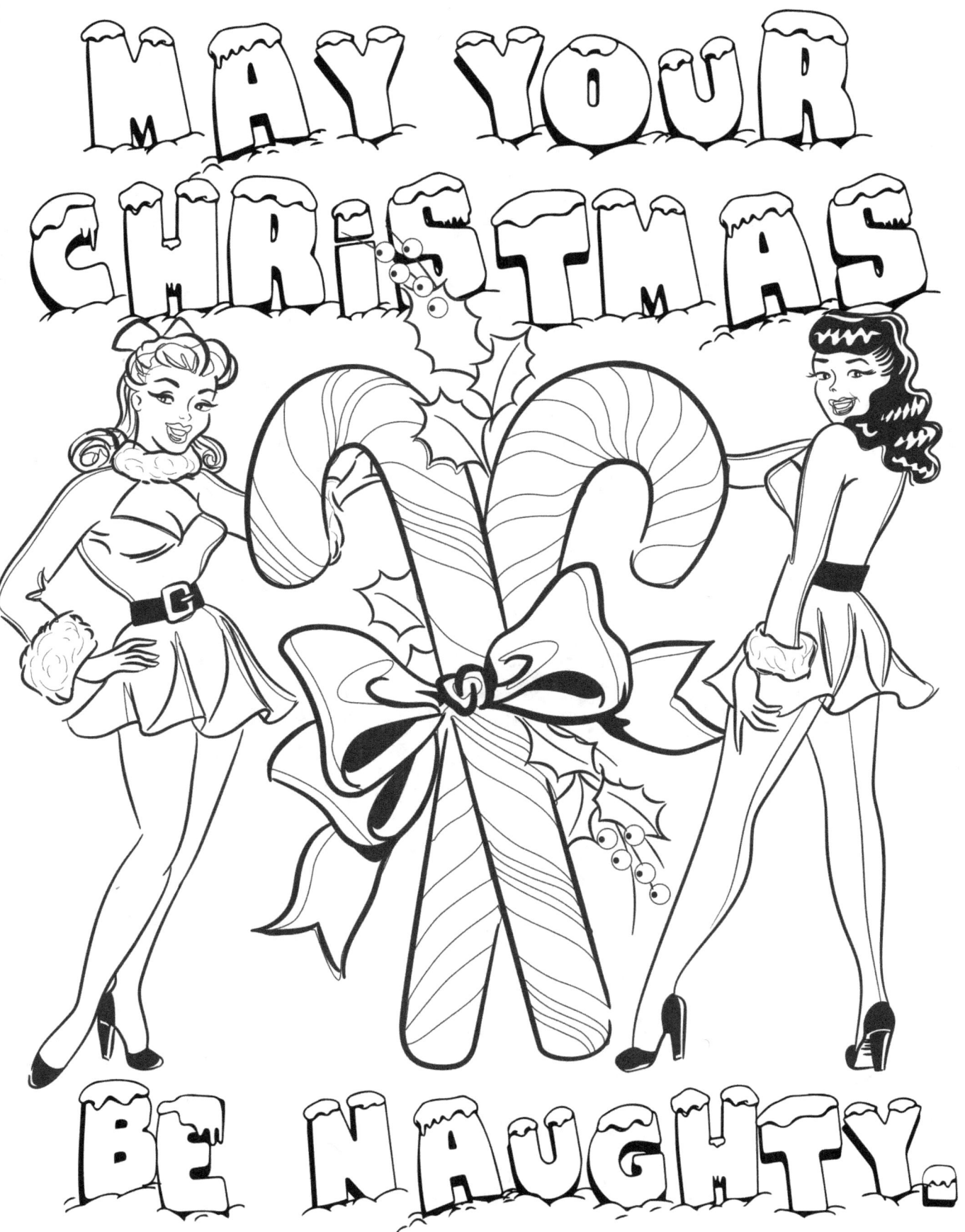

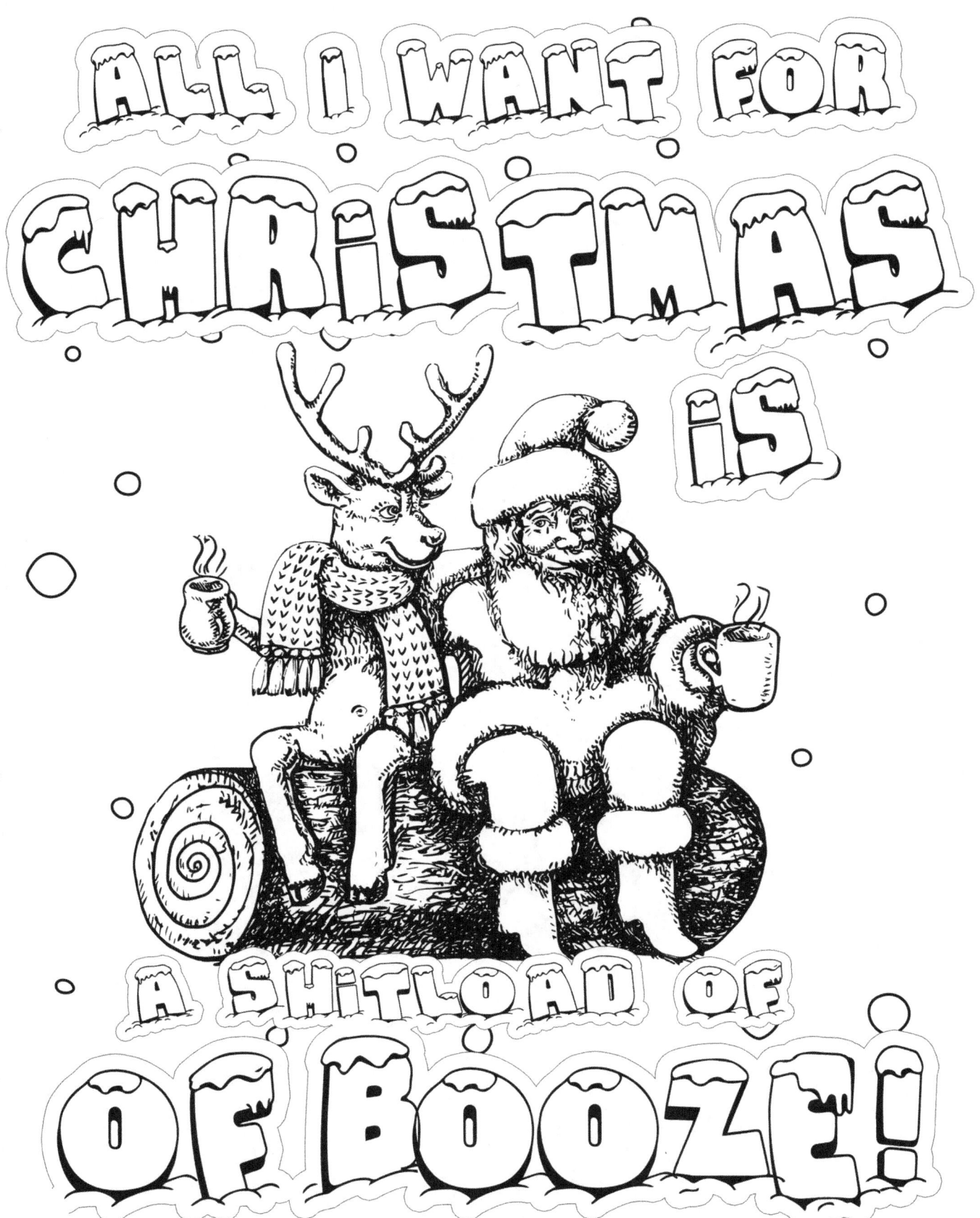

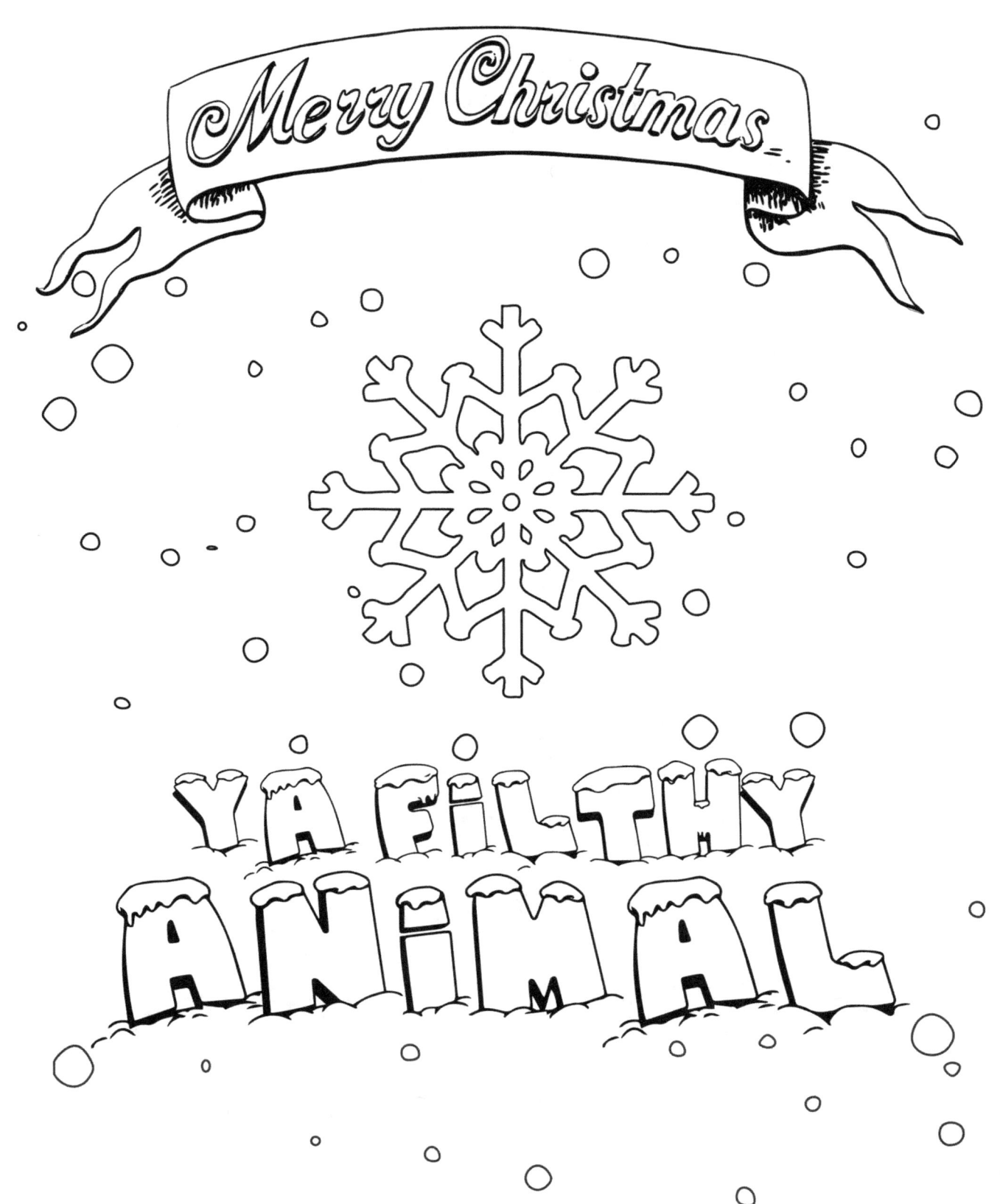

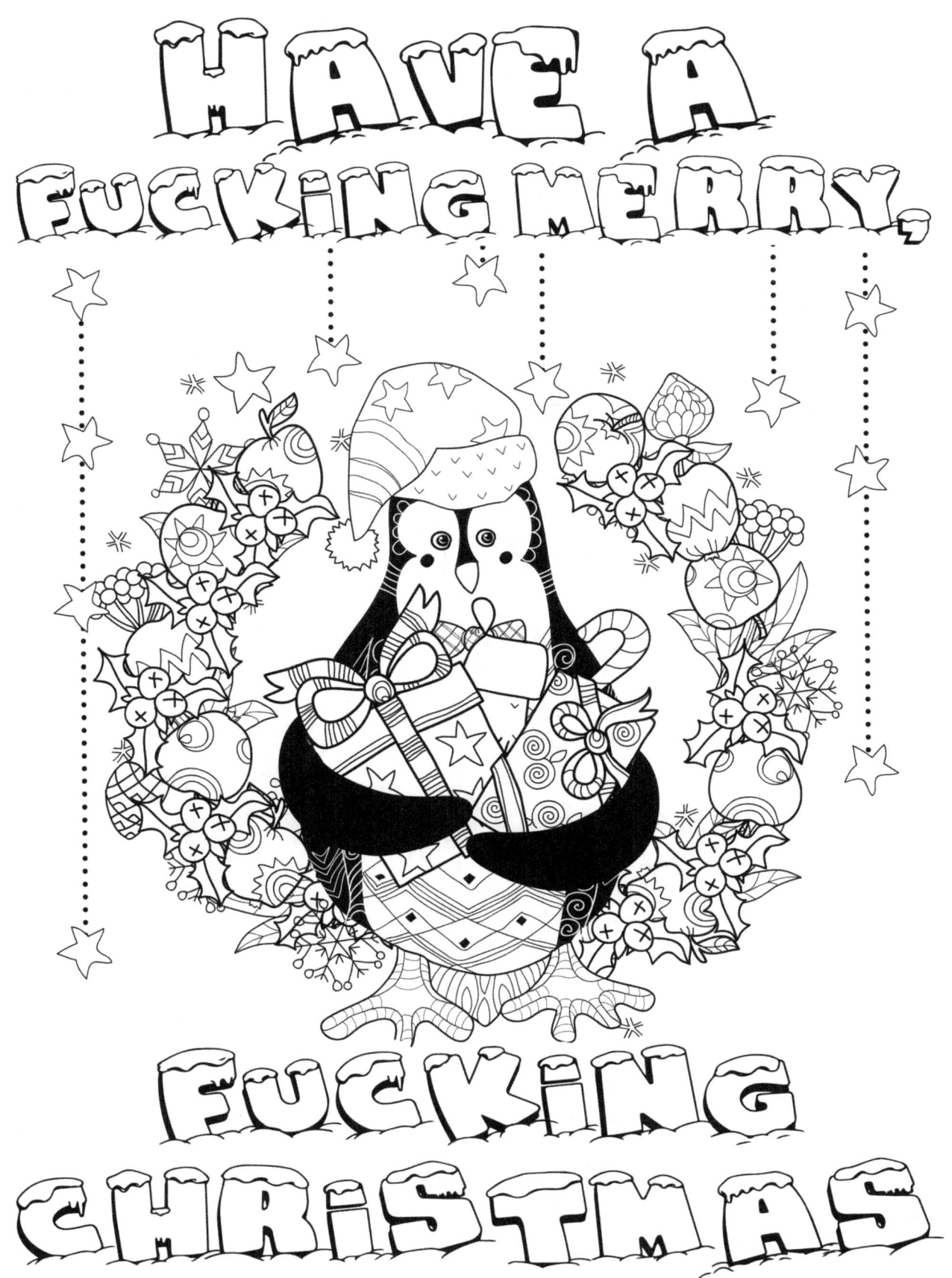

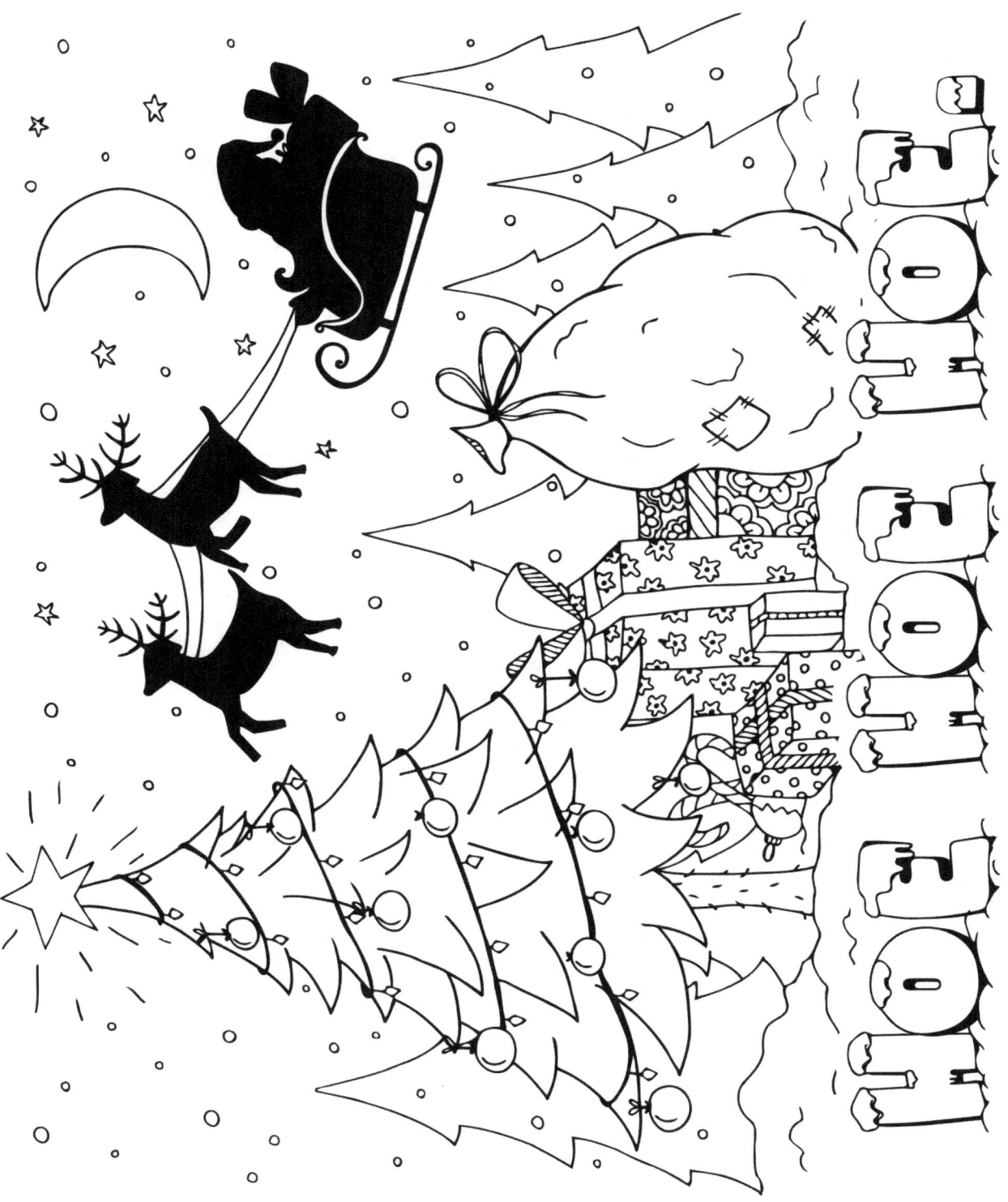

www.ingramcontent.com/pod-product-compliance
Lightning Source LLC
Chambersburg PA
CBHW062156220526
45470CB00009B/2841